BRASS AMERICA™

Quality Replacement Parts

A DIVISION OF: **BARRY E. WALTER SR. CO.**

REV. 2C

Quality Replacement Parts

Table of Contents

o Terms ii

o Index by Category iii

o Parts Listing 1

o Index by Part Number 71

o Index Button Cross Reference 81

Quality Replacement Parts

TERMS AND CONDITIONS OF SALE

SALES POLICY:
It is our policy to sell the OEM and wholesale level only. Possession of this book does not constitute an offer to sell. Prices are subject to change without notice. All orders will be shipped and invoiced at the prevailing price at the time of shipment. We reserve the right to adjust orders to standard package quantities unless otherwise stated on purchase order. All orders are subject to acceptance by Barry E. Walter Sr. Co., 2550 E. Platte Ave., Fort Morgan, CO 80701. The Minimum billing is $50.00. Drop shipments will carry a 10% surcharge and must meet minimum requirements.

TERMS:
3% 20, Net 30. Payment must be received within 20 days of the invoice date for the discount to be allowed. Any amount past due is subject to finance charge on the total past due balance in accordance with the truth-in-lending act. Invoices not paid according to the terms are subject to MONTHLY SERVICE CHARGES of 1 1/2% per month (which is an ANNUAL PERCENTAGE RATE OF 18%). Returned checks (NSF) will be charged a $25.00 handling charge. Prices are subject to any federal, state, sales use or other tax applying, unless exemption certificates are on file with Barry E. Walter Sr. Co. Cancellation of regular merchandise orders can be authorized only by Barry E. Walter Sr. Co. Handling charges may be assessed for canceled orders.

FREIGHT:
All orders will be shipped FOB Fort Morgan, Colorado.

RETURNS:
No goods will be accepted for return unless authorized by Barry E. Walter Sr. Co. in advance of return. Return goods are subject to a minimum 20% handling charge plus freight. All material returned without prior written permission will be assessed a minimum of 50% plus freight.

CLAIMS:
Claims for shortage must be made within five days after receipt of shipment. Items defective in material or workmanship will be replaced without charge. It is expressly understood that Barry E. Walter Sr. Co., liability is limited to furnishing of such replacement parts and that Barry E. Walter Sr. Co. will not be liable for any damages, losses, or expenses arising in connection with the use of or inability to use our products for any purpose.

SPECIAL MATERIAL:
Materials made to the specifications of the customers by Barry E. Walter Sr. Co. are not returnable. Once an order has been placed it cannot be canceled. Barry E. Walter Sr. Co. reserves the right to charge a $50.00 research fee to identify and quote on customer special requests.

GENERAL:
Barry E. Walter Sr. Co. represents that it has complied with the Fair Labor Standards Act of 1938, as amended, and the Fair Employment Practice Act. All Catalogs, Price List, and Production Information Publications remain the property of Barry E. Walter Sr. Co. We also stock many items which are not currently included in our catalog and are constantly adding replacement parts. If you don't find the item you need, just ask!

PRICING:

All Abrass items are net pricing.

Any usage of original manufactures' names or numbers, product names, and model names or numbers on invoices, quotes, or packing slips are strictly for descriptive and identification purposes. All drawing representations or depictions of original manufactures' products in Barry E. Walter Sr. Co. catalogs or faxes are strictly for identification purposes, and are used to determine the proper Barry Walter Co. replacement part. They are not meant to imply that the parts are manufactured by the original equipment manufacturer.

Index by Category

A

Acrylic Handles...5, 8, 11, 12, 18, 19, 20, 23, 28, 32
ADA Handles.....2, 6, 8, 9, 10, 11, 15, 30
Aerators................................37
American Brass*
  Brass Stems 1
  Chrome Plated Handles.....................1
  Diverter Handles 1
  Diverter Stems 1
  Faucet Handles..............................1
  Faucet Stems................................1
  Index Buttons 24
American Standard*
  ADA Handles 2
  Brass Stems 1
  Chrome Plated Escutcheons 3, 4
  Chrome Plated Handles............1, 2, 3
  Chrome Plated Stems 1
  Diverter Handles 2, 3
  Diverter Stems 1
  Escutcheon Sleeves 4
  Faucet Handles.....................1, 2, 3
  Faucet Seat Washers 4
  Faucet Stems................................1
  Index Buttons 4, 13
  Lock Nuts 1
  Screw On Disks 42
  Single Lever Handles......................3
  Snap On Disks 42
  Sponge Gaskets 42
  Tub & Shower Handles..............1, 2, 3
  Valve Seals 42
Angle Stop Supply Stop..............37, 38

B

Backflow Replacement Kits..............10
Ball Assemblies
  Brass Ball Assemblies 8, 9
  Stainless Steel Ball Assemblies......8, 9
Barrels...16, 29
Basin Cock Faucets 44
Bevel Washers...............................42
Binford
  Basin Cock Faucets 44
  Brass Grid Drains 44
  Chrome Plated Handles..................36
  Deck Mount Faucets..................43, 44
  Deck Mount Pantry Faucets.............44

  Deck Mount Pre-Rinse Units 44
  Diverter Stems.............................37
  Drain Pop-Up Assemblies 44
  Faucet Handles............................36
  Grid Drains 44
  Kitchen Faucets......................43, 44
  Lavatory Faucets 43, 44
  Loop Handles 36
  Pop-Up Plugs 44
  Pop-Up Stoppers 44
  Service Sink Faucets 43
  Tub & Shower Faucets 43, 44
  Tub & Shower Handle Kits 36, 45-70
  Wall Mount Faucets 43, 44
  Wall Mount Pre-Rinse Units 44
  Washerless Cartridges 37
Bolts
  Toilet Seat Bolts 41
Boot
  Diverter Stem Boot 37
Boxes
  Flapper Boxes 41
Brass Ball Assembly......................8, 9
Brass Barrels...........................16, 29
Brass Cartridges 19
Brass Grid Drains.........................44
Brass Nipples 14, 31
Brass Stem Assemblies 29
Brass Stems .. 1, 4, 5, 6, 7, 9, 14, 15, 16, 17, 19, 20, 21, 22, 24, 25, 26, 27, 28, 29, 30, 31
Briggs*
  Acrylic Handles...............................5
  Brass Stems 4
  Chrome Plated Handles 4
  Chrome Plated Stems 4
  Faucet Handles 4, 5
  Faucet Stems 4
  Index Buttons 4
  Plastic Cartridges 4
  Rubber Gaskets............................4
  Single Lever Cartridges 4
  Single Lever Handles 4
Bubbler Heads
  Drinking Fountain Bubbler Heads.....37
Buttons
  Index Buttons...4, 7, 8, 13, 14, 15, 16, 18, 24, 26, 28, 29, 30, 32

C

Cartridge Drains.............................. 40
Cartridges
  Brass Cartridges 19
  Ceramic Cartridges 33, 34, 35, 36
  Plastic Cartridges .. 4, 7, 14, 17, 18, 19, 20, 21, 31, 32, 33, 34, 35, 36, 37
  Plastic Ceramic Cartridges.. 33, 34, 35, 36
  Single Lever Cartridges... 4, 18, 19, 20, 21, 31, 32, 33, 34, 35, 36
  Tub & Shower Cartridges...4, 18, 19, 20, 21, 22, 31, 32, 33, 34, 35, 36
  Washerless Cartridges...7, 14, 17, 18, 19, 20, 31, 32, 33, 37
Central Brass*
  Brass Stems.............................. 5
  Chrome Plated Escutcheons............ 6
  Chrome Plated Handles 5, 6
  Chrome Plated Stems 5
  Diverter Handles 5, 6
  Diverter Stems 5
  Faucet Handles 5, 6
  Faucet Stems 5
  Tub & Shower Handles 5, 6
Ceramic Cartridges... 16, 21, 22, 26, 30, 33, 34, 35, 36
Ceramic Disc Stems . 16, 21, 22, 26, 30, 33, 34, 35, 36
CFG*
  Ceramic Cartridges 35
  Single Lever Cartridges................... 35
CHG*
  Chrome Plated Handles 6
  Faucet Stems 6
  Hot & Cold Stems............................ 6
Chicago*
  ADA Handles............................. 6
  Chrome Plated Handles 6
  Chrome Plated Stems 6
  Faucet Handles 6
  Faucet Stems 6
  Index Rings 6
Chrome Plated Escutcheons . 3, 4, 6, 8, 12, 13, 15, 16, 18, 19, 20, 21, 23, 24, 25, 26, 27, 31
Chrome Plated Handles...1, 2, 3, 4, 5, 6, 7, 8, 9, 10, 11, 14, 15, 16, 17, 18, 19, 22, 23, 25, 26, 27, 29, 30, 31, 32, 36

Index by Category

Quality Replacement Parts

Chrome Plated Stems...1, 4, 5, 6, 9, 16, 17, 21, 24, 26, 29
Chrome Shower heads......................40
Closet Spuds 41
Coast*
  Vinyl Flappers 41
Concinnity*
  Ceramic Cartridges 34
  Single Lever Cartridges 34
Connectors
  Shower Arm Connectors.................40
Crane*
  Brass Stems 6, 7
  Chrome Plated Handles.....................7
  Diverter Handles...........................7
  Diverter Stems............................7
  Faucet Handles............................7
  Faucet Stems...........................6, 7
  Index Buttons.............................7
  Tub & Shower Handles......................7
Cushions
  Rubber Cushions 42

D

Deck Mount Faucets................43, 44
Deck Mount Pantry Faucets 44
Deck Mount Pre-Rinse Units 44
Delta*
  Acrylic Handles 8
  ADA Handles 8
  Brass Ball Assemblies 8, 9
  Chrome Plated Escutcheons 8
  Chrome Plated Handles.....................8
  Extensions Stems 7, 8
  Faucet Ball Assemblies..................8, 9
  Faucet Handles..............................8
  Faucet Stems..............................7
  Handle Repair Kits..........................8
  Index Buttons.............................8
  Plastic Cartridges..........................7
  Push/Pull Diverter Cartridges..............7
  Seat/Spring Repair Kits.....................9
  Single Lever Ball Assemblies..........8, 9
  Single Lever Handles.......................8
  Stainless Steel Ball Assemblies......8, 9
  Stem Extensions 7, 8
  Tub & Shower Handles......................8
  Washerless Cartridges......................7

Disks
  Screw On Disks...............................42
  Snap On Disks................................42
Disposal Stoppers......................42
Diverter Cartridges
  Ceramic Diverter Cartridges 33
  Push/Pull Diverter Cartridges 7
Diverter Gates
  Tub Spout Diverter Gates.................38
Diverter Handles...1, 2, 3, 5, 6, 7, 9, 10, 14, 15, 16, 17, 18, 22, 23, 25, 26, 27, 28, 30, 31
Diverter Stem Boots......................37
Diverter Stems...1, 5, **7**, 9, 14, 15, 17, 21, 22, 25, 26, 30, 31, 37
Diverter Tub Spouts......................39
Diverters
  Spray Diverters...............................43
Drain Pop-Up Assemblies 44
Drains
  Cartridge Drains 44
  Grid Drains 44
  Tub & Shower Drains 39
Drinking Fountain Parts
  Bubbler Head 37
  Cartridge 37

E

Eljer*
  ADA Handles 9
  Brass Stems 9
  Chrome Plated Handles 9, 10
  Chrome Plated Stems 9
  Diverter Handles..........................9, 10
  Diverter Stems................................9
  Faucet Handles 9, 10
  Faucet Stems 9
  Flush Handles 40
  Tub & Shower Handles.................9, 10
Elkay*
  Cartridge Drinking Fountains...........37
Escutcheon Sleeves...4, 13, 15, 16, 24, 25, 26, 28, 31
Escutcheons
  Chrome Plated Escutcheons...3, 4, 6, 8, 12, 13, 15, 16, 18, 19, 20, 21, 23, 24, 25, 26, 27, 31
  Spray Escutcheons..........................37

Extensions
  Stem Extensions 7, 8, 20
EZ-Flo*
  Ceramic Cartridges 33, 34, 35
  Single Lever Cartridges........ 33, 34, 35

F

Face Plates
  Overflow Face Plates 39
  Trip Lever Face Plates 23, 39
Faucet ADA Handles .. 2, 6, 8, 9, 10, 11, 15, 30
Faucet Ball Assemblies................... 8, 9
Faucet Handles...1, 2, 3, 4, 5, 6, 7, 8, 9, 10, 11, 12, 14, 15, 16, 17, 18, 19, 20, 22, 23, 25, 26, 27, 28, 29, 30, 31, 32, 36
Faucet Seat Washers..................... 4, 24
Faucet Spray Nozzles..................... 37
Faucet Stems...1, 2, 3, 4, 6, 7, 9, 14, 15, 16, 17, 18, 19, 20, 21, 22, 24, 25, 26, 27, 28, 29, 30, 31, 32, 33,37
Faucet Supply Stops 37, 38
Faucets
  Basin Cock Faucets 44
  Deck Mount Faucets 43, 44
  Deck Mount Pantry Faucets............ 44
  Kitchen Faucets 43, 44
  Lavatory Faucets 43, 44
  Pre-Rinse Faucets 44
  Service Sink Faucets 43
  Tub & Shower Faucets................ 43, 44
  Wall Mount Faucets 43, 44
Febco*
  Backflow Replacement Kits............. 10
  Gasket Repair Kits 10
Fisher*
  Faucet Handles............................ 14
Fit-All
  Acrylic Handles 11, 12
  ADA Handles............................ 10, 11
  Brass Nipples 14
  Chrome Plated Escutcheons...... 12, 13
  Chrome Plated Handles 10, 11
  Escutcheon Sleeves........................ 13
  Faucet Handles 10, 11, 12
  Fit-All Nipples 13
  Index Buttons 13, 14, 26
  Plastic Tapered Nipples 13

To Order Call: 1.800.767.5552 . Fax: 1.800.886.9831

Original Mfg's names are used for identification only and are not a representation that the items offered are genuine items of the original Mfg.   *iv*

Quality Replacement Parts

Index by Category

Threaded Nipples 13, 14
Tub & Shower Handles 10, 11, 12
Flapper Boxes 41
Flappers
Rubber Flappers 41
Toilet Flappers 41
Vinyl Flappers 41
Flat Stoppers 42
Flat Washers 42
Flush Handles 40

G

Gasket Repair Kits 10
Gaskets
Rubber Gaskets 4, 42
Sponge Gaskets 42
Gerber*
ADA Handles 15
Balancing Spool 36
Brass Stems 14
Ceramic Cartridges 36
Chrome Plated Escutcheons 15
Chrome Plated Handles 14, 15
Diverter Handles 14, 15
Diverter Stems 14
Escutcheon Sleeves 15
Faucet Handles 14, 15
Faucet Stems 14
Index Buttons 13, 15
Plastic Cartridges 14
Single Lever Cartridges 36
Single Lever Mixing Spools 36
Tub & Shower Handles 14, 15
Washerless Cartridges 14
Glacier Bay*
Ceramic Cartridges 33
Ceramic Disc Stems 33
Faucet Stems 33
Single Lever Cartridges 33
Grid Drains
Brass Grid Drains 44

H

Handle & Stem Assemblies 29
Handle Repair Kits
Acrylic Handles...5, 8, 11, 12, 18, 19,
20, 23, 28, 32
ADA Handles...2, 6, 8, 9, 10, 11, 15, 30

Chrome Plated Handles...1, 2, 3, 4, 5,
6, 7, 8, 9, 10, 11, 14, 15, 16, 17, 18,
19, 22, 23, 25, 26, 27, 29, 30, 31,
32, 36
Diverter Handles...1, 2, 3, 5, 6, 7, 9, 10,
14, 15, 16, 17, 18, 22, 23, 25, 26,
27, 28, 30, 31
Faucet Handles...1, 2, 3, 4, 5, 6, 7, 8, 9,
10, 11, 12, 14, 15, 16, 17, 18, 19,
20, 22, 23, 25, 26, 27, 28, 29, 30,
31, 32, 36
Flush Handles 40
Lavatory Handles... 1, 2, 3, 5, 6, 7, 8, 9,
10, 11, 12, 14, 15, 16, 17, 18, 19,
20, 22, 23, 25, 26, 27, 28, 29, 30,
31, 32, 36
Lever Handles...2, 3, 6, 7, 8, 9, 10, 11,
14, 15, 16, 17, 19, 22, 23, 27, 29,
30, 31, 32, 36
Loop Handles 36
Single Lever Handles...3, 4, 8, 19, 20,
23, 29, 32, 36
Tub & Shower Handles...1, 2, 3, 5, 6, 7,
8, 9, 10, 11, 12, 14, 15, 16, 17, 18,
19, 20, 22, 23, 25, 26, 27, 28, 29,
30, 31, 32, 36
Wall Hydrant Handles 32
Harcraft*
Brass Stems 15
Chrome Plated Escutcheons 16
Chrome Plated Handles 15
Diverter Stems 15
Faucet Stems 15
Index Buttons 16
Tub & Shower Handles 15
Harrington*
Ceramic Cartridges 34
Single Lever Cartridges 34
Haws*
Drinking Fountain Bubbler Heads 37
Heads
Tub & Shower Heads 40
Hoses
Pre-Rinse Hoses 37
Huntington*
Ceramic Cartridges 34
Single Lever Cartridges 34
Hydroplast
Ceramic Cartridges 34, 35
Single Lever Cartridges 34, 35

I

Import Ceramic Cartridges 33, 34, 35
Index Buttons...4, 7, 8, 13, 14, 15, 16, 18,
24, 26, 28, 29, 30, 32
Index Rings 6, 30
Indiana Brass*
Brass Stems 16
Chrome Plated Handles 16
Diverter Handles 16
Escutcheon Sleeves 16
Faucet Handles 16
Faucet Stems 16
Tub & Shower Handles 16

J

Jaclo*
Ceramic Cartridges 34
Single Lever Cartridges 34
Jado*
Ceramic Cartridges 33
Single Lever Cartridges 33

K

Kit Seats 9, 32
Kitchen Faucet Spray Diverters 43
Kitchen Faucets 43, 44
Kohler*
Acrylic Handles 18
Brass Barrels 16
Brass Stems 16, 17
Ceramic Disc Stems 16
Chrome Plated Escutcheons 18
Chrome Plated Handles 17, 18
Chrome Plated Stems 16, 17
Diverter Handles 17, 18
Diverter Stems 17
Faucet Handles 17, 18
Faucet Stems 16, 17
Flush Handles 40
Index Buttons 18
Plastic Cartridges 17
Plastic Nipples................... 18
Single Lever Cartridges 34
Threaded Nipples................ 18
Tub & Shower Handles 17, 18
Washerless Cartridges 17

L

Index by Category

Quality Replacement Parts

Lavatory Faucets............................43, 44
Lavatory Handles...1, 2, 3, 5, 6, 7, 8, 9,
    10, 11, 12, 14, 15, 16, 17, 18, 19, 20,
    22, 23, 25, 26, 27, 28, 29, 30, 31, 32,
    36
Lever Handles...2, 3, 6, 7, 8, 9, 10, 11,
    14, 15, 16, 17, 19, 22, 23, 27, 29, 30,
    31, 32, 36
Loop Handles......................................36

M

Male Aerators......................................37
Milwaukee*
    Brass Stems 19
    Faucet Stems.......................................18
    Plastic Cartridges..............................18
    Washerless Cartridges......................18
Mixet*
    Acrylic Handles 19
    Chrome Plated Escutcheons 19
    Chrome Plated Handles..............19, 36
    Faucet Handles....................................36
    Faucet Stems.......................................19
    Loop Handles.................................19, 36
    Single Lever Cartridges 19
    Single Lever Handles..................19, 36
    Tub & Shower Handles...............19, 36
Mixing Spools
    Single Lever Mixing Spools...............36
Moen*
    Acrylic Handles 20
    Chrome Plated Handles.....................19
    Diverter Handles 19
    Faucet Handles....................................20
    Faucet Stems.......................................19
    Plastic Cartridges..............................19
    Single Lever Cartridges 19
    Single Lever Handles.........................20
    Tub & Shower Handles...............19, 20
    Washerless Cartridges......................19

N

Niagara*
    Tub & Shower Heads..........................40
Nibco*
    Acrylic Handles 20
    Cartridges 20
    Chrome Plated Escutcheons 20
    Escutcheon Extension 20

    Faucet Handles 20
    Faucet Stems 20
    Plastic Cartridges 20
    Single Lever Cartridges 20
    Stem Extension 20
    Washerless Cartridges 20
Nipples
    Brass Nipples 14, 31
    Fit-All Nipples 13
    Plastic Nipples...............13, 18, 24, 28
    Plastic Tapered Nipples....................13
    Threaded Nipples..13, 14, 18, 24, 28, 31
Nuts
    Lock Nuts 1
    Slip Joint Nuts 40

P

Paijo*
    Ceramic Cartridges............................34
    Single Lever Cartridges 34
Pegasus*
    Ceramic Cartridges............................34
    Single Lever Cartridges 34
Phoenix*
    Acrylic Handles...................................20
    Brass Stems 20
    Chrome Plated Escutcheons 21
    Faucet Stems 20
    Tub & Shower Handles.......................20
Plastic Cartridges...4, 7, 14, 17, 18, 19,
    20, 21, 31, 32, 33, 34, 35, 36, 37
Plastic Ceramic Cartridges...33, 34, 35,
    36
Plastic Nipples 13, 18, 24, 28
Plastic Tapered Nipples....................13
Plugs
    Pop-Up Plugs 44
    Test Plugs 40
Pop-Up Assemblies
    Drain Pop-Up Assemblies 44
Pop-Up Plugs.......................................44
Pop-Up Stoppers.................................44
Premier*
    Diverter Stem Boots 37
Pre-Rinse Faucets
    Deck Mount Pre-Rinse Faucets........44
    Wall Mount Pre-Rinse Faucets........44
Pre-Rinse Hoses.................................30
Pre-Rinse Spray Heads....................30

Pre-Rinse Springs.............................. 30
Price Pfister*
    Acrylic Handles 23
    Brass Stems................................ 21, 22
    Ceramic Cartridges 33, 35
    Ceramic Disc Stems.................... 21, 22
    Chrome Plated Escutcheons...... 23, 24
    Chrome Plated Handles 22, 23
    Chrome Plated Stems 21
    Diverter Handles 22, 23
    Diverter Stems 21, 22
    Escutcheon Sleeves.......................... 24
    Faucet Handles 22, 23
    Faucet Seat Washers........................ 24
    Faucet Stems 21, 22
    Index Buttons 7, 13, 24
    Plastic Cartridges 21
    Plastic Nipples.................................. 24
    Single Lever Cartridges........ 21, 33, 35
    Single Lever Handles 23
    Threaded Nipples............................. 24
    Trip Lever Face Plates 23
    Tub & Shower Handles 22, 23
Pro Flo*
    Ceramic Cartridges 35
    Single Lever Cartridges.................... 35
Push/Pull Diverter Cartridges 7

R

Repair Kits
    Seat/Spring Repair Kits................ 9, 32
    Tub & Shower 45-70
Replacement Kits
    Backflow Replacement Kits.............. 10
    Gasket Repair Kits 10
Rings
    Index Rings 6, 30
    Tub & Shower Rings 36
Rubber Cushions............................... 42
Rubber Flappers 41
Rubber Gaskets 4, 42

To Order Call: 1.800.767.5552 . Fax: 1.800.886.9831

Original Mfg's names are used for identification only and are not a representation that the items offered are genuine items of the original Mfg.   *vi*

Index by Category

S

Savoy*
Brass Stems 24, 25
Chrome Plated Escutcheons 25
Chrome Plated Handles....................25
Chrome Plated Stems......................24
Diverter Handles 25
Diverter Stems 25
Escutcheon Sleeves 25
Faucet Handles 25
Faucet Stems............................24, 25

Sayco*
Balancing Spool..............................36
Brass Stems 25
Ceramic Cartridges.....................33, 35
Chrome Plated Escutcheons 26
Chrome Plated Handles........25, 26, 36
Diverter Handles 25
Diverter Stems 25
Escutcheon Sleeves 26
Faucet Handles....................25, 26, 36
Faucet Stems 26
Index Buttons 26
Single Lever Cartridges 33, 35
Single Lever Handles......................36
Single Lever Mixing Spools..............36
Tub & Shower Handles.........25, 26, 36

Screw On Disks 42

Seals
Valve Seals....................................42

Seasons*
Ceramic Cartridges.........................34
Single Lever Cartridges 34

Seat/Spring Repair Kits................9, 32

Service Sink Faucets 43

Shower Arm Connectors 40

Shower Arms 40

Showers Heads............................40

Single Lever
Single Lever Ball Assemblies..........8, 9
Single Lever Cartridges...4, 18, 19, 20,
21, 31, 32, 33, 34, 35, 36
Single Lever Handles...3, 4, 8, 19, 20,
23, 29, 32, 36
Single Lever Mixing Spools..............36

Sink & Tubs Stoppers......................42

Sink Spray Hoses 37

Sleeves
Escutcheon Sleeves...4, 13, 15, 16, 24,
25, 26, 28, 31

Slip Joint Nuts................................40

Slip Joints Washers 42

Snap On Disks................................42

Speakman*
Ceramic Disc Stems 26
Chrome Plated Handles 26
Chrome Plated Stems 26
Diverter Handles............................26
Faucet Stems 26
Index Buttons 13

Sponge Gaskets............................42

Spouts
Tub Spouts 38, 39

Spray Diverters
Kitchen Faucet Spray Diverters........43

Spray Escutcheons..........................37

Spray Hoses
Sink Spray Hoses...........................37

Spray Nozzles
Faucet Spray Nozzles 37

Spuds
Closet Spuds 41
Urinal Spuds 41

Stainless Steel Ball Assemblies 8, 9

Starlight*
Ceramic Cartridges.........................35
Single Lever Cartridges 35

Stem
Brass Stems 1

Stem Assemblies
Brass Stem Assemblies..................29

Stem Extensions 7, 8, 20

Stem Sleeves................................7, 8

Stems
Brass Stems...1, 4, 5, 6, 7, 9, 14, 15,
16, 17, 19, 20, 21, 22, 24, 25, 26,
27, 28, 29, 30, 31
Ceramic Disc Stems...16, 21, 22, 26,
30, 33, 34, 35, 36
Chrome Plated Stems...1, 4, 5, 9, 16,
17, 19, 21, 24, 26, 29
Diverter Stems...1, 5, 7, 9, 14, 15, 17,
21, 22, 25, 26, 30, 31, 37
Faucet Stems...1, 2, 3, 4, 6, 14, 15, 16,
17, 18, 19, 20, 21, 22, 24, 25, 26,
27, 28, 29, 30, 31, 32, 33,37

Sterling*
Acrylic Handles 28
Brass Stems 26, 27
Chrome Plated Escutcheons...........28
Chrome Plated Handles 27
Chrome Plated Stems 26
Diverter Handles 27, 28
Diverter Stems 26
Escutcheon Sleeves 27
Faucet Handles........................27, 28
Faucet Stems 26, 27
Index Buttons 13, 28
Plastic Nipples 28
Threaded Nipples 28
Tub & Shower Handles 27, 28

Stoppers
Disposal Stoppers 42
Flat Stoppers 42
Pop-Up Stoppers............................44
Sink & Tubs Stoppers 42

Streamway*
Brass Stems..................................28
Chrome Plated Handles 29
Faucet Handles..............................29
Faucet Stems 28

Supply Stops............................37, 38

Symmons*
Ceramic Cartridges 33
Chrome Plated Handles 29
Faucet Handles..............................29
Index Buttons 29
Single Lever Cartridges..................33
Single Lever Handles......................29
Tub & Shower Handles 29

T

Tank to Bowl Gaskets 42

T & S*
ADA Handles..................................30
Brass Barrels.................................29
Brass Stem Assemblies 29
Brass Stems..................................29
Chrome Plated Handles 29, 30
Chrome Plated Stems 29
Diverter Handles 30
Faucet Handles........................29, 30
Faucet Stems 29
Index Buttons 30
Index Rings 30
Pre-Rinse Hoses 30

Original Mfg's names are used for identification only and are not a representation that the items offered are genuine items of the original Mfg.

Index by Category

BRASS AMERICA
Quality Replacement Parts

Pre-Rinse Spray Heads 30
Pre-Rinse Springs............................30
Tub & Shower Handles 29, 30
Tub & Shower Handles ADA............30
Vacuum Breaker Kit.........................30
Tapered Plastic Nipples 13
Test Plugs 40
Threaded Nipples...13, 14, 18, 24, 28, 31
Toilet Flappers...................................41
Toilet Seat Bolts 41
Trip Lever Face Plates 23, 39
Tub & Shower Cartridges...4, 18, 19, 20,
    21, 22, 31, 32, 33, 34, 35, 36
Tub & Shower Drains 39
Tub & Shower Faucets.................43, 44
Tub & Shower Handle & Stem
    Assemblies 45-70
Tub & Shower Handles...1, 2, 3, 5, 6, 7,
    8, 9, 10, 11, 12, 14, 15, 16, 17, 18,
    19, 20, 22, 23, 25, 26, 27, 28, 29, 30,
    31, 32, 36
Tub & Shower Heads.........................40
Tub & Shower Repair Kits 45-70
Tub & Shower Rings 36
Tub Spout Diverter Gates 38
Tub Spouts
    Diverter Tub Spouts..........................39

U

Union Brass*
    Brass Nipples..................................31
    Brass Stems 30, 31
    Ceramic Disc Stems 30
    Chrome Plated Escutcheons 31
    Chrome Plated Handles....................31
    Diverter Handles 31
    Diverter Stems 30, 31
    Escutcheon Sleeves 31
    Faucet Handles................................31
    Faucet Stems...............................30, 31
    Handle Diverters 31
    Threaded Nipples 31
    Tub & Shower Handles 31
Urinal Spuds 41

V

Valley*
    Acrylic Handles 32
    Chrome Plated Handles....................32

Faucet Handles 32
Faucet Stems 31, 32
Index Buttons 32
Plastic Cartridges 31, 32
Seat/Spring Repair Kits 32
Single Lever Cartridges 31, 32
Single Lever Handles 32
Tub & Shower Handles.....................32
Washerless Cartridges 31, 32
Valve Seals 42
Vinyl Flappers 41

W

Wall Hydrant Handles 32
Wall Mount Faucets 43, 44
Wall Mount Pre-Rinse Units 44
Washerless Cartridges...7, 14, 17, 18,
    19, 31, 32, 37
Washers
    Bevel Washers 42
    Flat Washers 42
    Slip Joints Washers.........................42
Wolverine
    Ceramic Cartridges....................35, 36
    Single Lever Cartridges 35, 36
Woodford*
    Wall Hydrant Handles......................32

Z

Zurn*
    Ceramic Cartridges..........................34
    Single Lever Cartridges 34

To Order Call: 1.800.767.5552 . Fax: 1.800.886.9831

Original Mfg's names are used for identification only and are not a representation that the items offered are genuine items of the original Mfg. *viii*

Quality Replacement Parts

Quality Replacement Parts

AMERICAN BRASS*

Stem

Brass

- 20 TPI
- Includes gasket

Item #	Length (in)	Broach	H/C
ABRAM20176-LF	2 9/16	3-7 (17pt)	H or C

AMERICAN BRASS*

Diverter Stem

Brass

Item #	Length (in)	TPI	Broach
ABRAM20177	3 15/16	20	3-7 (17pt)

AMERICAN BRASS*

Handle Pair

Chrome

- Also fits Nibco, Phoenix & Streamway

Item #	Height (in)	Broach
ABRAM33051	1 5/8	3-7 (17pt)

AMERICAN BRASS*

Diverter Handle

Chrome

- Also fits Nibco, Phoenix & Streamway

Item #	Height (in)	Broach
ABRAM33051D	1 5/8	3-7 (17pt)

AMERICAN STANDARD*

Stem

Brass

Aquaseal

NSF / ANSI 372 Compliant

Item #	Length (in)	Broach	H/C
ABRAS10101-LF	1 15/16	1-4 (22pt)	Hot
ABRAS10102-LF	1 15/16	1-4 (22pt)	Cold

AMERICAN STANDARD*

Stem

Brass

"R" Series

- Includes o-ring

NSF / ANSI 372 Compliant

Item #	Length (in)	Broach	H/C
ABRAS10103-LF	1 23/32	1-4 (22pt)	Hot
ABRAS10104-LF	1 23/32	1-4 (22pt)	Cold

AMERICAN STANDARD*

Lock Nut

Brass

Aquaseal

Item #	Height (in)
ABRAS10105	9/16

AMERICAN STANDARD*

Stem

Brass

Cadet

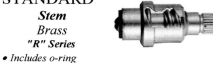

NSF / ANSI 372 Compliant

Item #	Length (in)	Broach	H/C
ABRAS10108-LF	1 9/32	1-6 (16pt)	Hot
ABRAS10109-LF	1 9/32	1-6 (16pt)	Cold

AMERICAN STANDARD*

Diverter Stem

Brass

Heritage

Item #	Length (in)	Broach
ABRAS20101	5 1/4	1-4 (22pt)

AMERICAN STANDARD*

Stem

Brass

Tract-Line

- Includes gasket

Item #	Length (in)	TPI	Broach
ABRAS20170-18T	5 1/4	18	1-4 (22pt)

AMERICAN STANDARD*

Stem

Brass

Colony

Item #	Length (in)	Broach	H/C
ABRAS20172	4 1/2	1-6 (16pt)	H or C

AMERICAN STANDARD*

Diverter Stem

Brass

Colony

Item #	Length (in)	Broach
ABRAS20173	5	1-6 (16pt)

AMERICAN STANDARD*

Stem

Brass

Colony

Item #	Length (in)	Broach	H/C
ABRAS20174	5	1-6 (16pt)	H or C

AMERICAN STANDARD*

Stem

Brass

Re-Nu

- Chrome plated stem, includes gasket

Item #	Length (in)	Broach	H/C
ABRAS20186-15	5 15/32	1-4 (22pt)	H or C

AMERICAN STANDARD*

Lav / Kit Handle pair

Chrome

Cadet

Item #	Height (in)	Broach
ABRAS32100	2 1/4	1-6 (16pt)

Quality Replacement Parts

AMERICAN STANDARD*
Tub & Shower Handle Pair
Chrome
Cadet

Item #	Height (in)	Broach
ABRAS32101	2 ¾	1-6 (16pt)

AMERICAN STANDARD*
Diverter Handle
Chrome
Cadet

Item #	Height (in)	Broach
ABRAS32101D	2 ¾	1-6 (16pt)

AMERICAN STANDARD*
ADA Lav/Kit Handle Pair
Chrome

• Includes chrome buttons

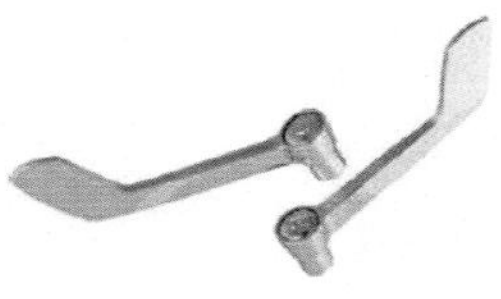

Item #	Length (in)	Broach
ABRAS32110	4 ¼	1-4 (22pt)

AMERICAN STANDARD*
Lav/Kit Handle Pair
Chrome
Colony

Item #	Height (in)	Broach
ABRAS32120	1 ³⁄₁₆	1-6 (16pt)

AMERICAN STANDARD*
Tub & Shower Handle Pair
Chrome
Colony

Item #	Height (in)	Broach
ABRAS32121	1 ¼	1-6 (16pt)

AMERICAN STANDARD*
Tub & Shower Handle Pair
Chrome
Colony

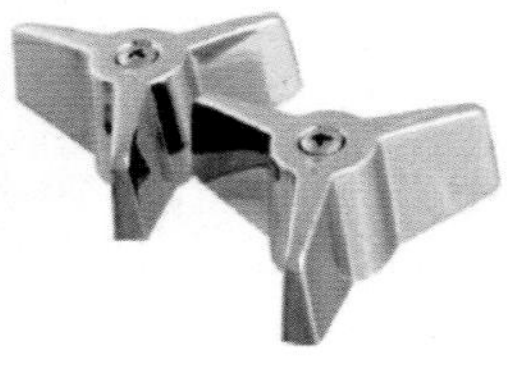

Item #	Height (in)	Broach
ABRAS32130	1 ⅛	1-6 (16pt)

AMERICAN STANDARD*
Diverter Handle
Chrome
Colony

Item #	Height (in)	Broach
ABRAS32130D	1 ⅛	1-6 (16pt)

AMERICAN STANDARD*
Lav/Kit Handle Pair
Chrome
Colony

Item #	Height (in)	Broach
ABRAS32131	1 ⅛	1-6 (16pt)

AMERICAN STANDARD*
Tub & Shower Handle Pair
Chrome
Colony

Item #	Height (in)	Broach
ABRAS32140	1 ⅛	1-6 (16pt)

AMERICAN STANDARD*
Diverter Handle
Chrome
Colony

Item #	Height (in)	Broach
ABRAS32140D	1 ⅛	1-6 (16pt)

AMERICAN STANDARD*
Handle Pair
Chrome
Colony Shelf

Item #	Height (in)	Broach
ABRAS32141	1 ¼	1-6 (16pt)

AMERICAN STANDARD*
Tub & Shower Handle Pair
Chrome
Heritage

Item #	Height (in)	Broach
ABRAS32170	1 ⅝	1-4 (22pt)

AMERICAN STANDARD*
Diverter Handle
Chrome
Heritage

Item #	Height (in)	Broach
ABRAS32170D	1 ⅝	1-4 (22pt)

AMERICAN STANDARD*
Lavatory Handle Pair
Chrome
Heritage

Item #	Height (in)	Broach
ABRAS32171	1 ⅝	1-4 (22pt)

AMERICAN STANDARD*
Tub & Shower Handle Pair
Chrome
Heritage, Aquaseal

Item #	Height (in)	Broach
ABRAS32172	1 ¹¹⁄₁₆	1-4 (22pt)

BRASS AMERICA
Quality Replacement Parts

AMERICAN STANDARD*
Diverter Handle
Chrome
Heritage, Aquaseal

Item #	Height (in)	Broach
ABRAS32172D	1 11/16	1-4 (22pt)

AMERICAN STANDARD*
Lavatory Handle
Chrome
Aquarian

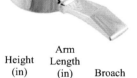

Item #	Height (in)	Arm Length (in)	Broach
ABRAS32173	1 1/16	2 3/8	▢

AMERICAN STANDARD*
Lavatory Handle Pair
Chrome
Heritage, Aquaseal

Item #	Height (in)	Broach
ABRAS32175	1 1/4	1-4 (22pt)

AMERICAN STANDARD*
Kitchen Handle
Chrome
Aquarian

Item #	Height (in)	Arm Length (in)	Broach
ABRAS32176	1 1/16	4 1/4	▢

AMERICAN STANDARD*
Tub & Shower Handle Pair
Chrome
Tackline

Item #	Height (in)	Broach
ABRAS32178	9/16	1-4 (22pt)

AMERICAN STANDARD*
Diverter Handle
Chrome
Tackline

Item #	Height (in)	Broach
ABRAS32178D	9/16	1-4 (22pt)

AMERICAN STANDARD*
Lav/Kit Handle
Chrome
Aquarian II

Item #	Height (in)	Length (in)	Broach
ABRAS32181	7/8	3	▢

AMERICAN STANDARD*
Lav/Kit Handle
Chrome
Ultramix

Item #	Height (in)	Length (in)	Broach
ABRAS32182	7/8	2 7/8	▭

AMERICAN STANDARD*
Tub & Shower Handle Pair
Chrome
Crown

Item #	Height (in)	Width (in)	Broach
ABRAS32183	1 7/8	2 5/8	1-4 (22pt)

AMERICAN STANDARD*
Diverter Handle
Chrome
Crown

Item #	Height (in)	Width (in)	Broach
ABRAS32183D	1 7/8	2 5/8	1-4 (22pt)

AMERICAN STANDARD*
Lav/Kit Handle Pair
Chrome
Heritage

Item #	Height (in)	Broach
ABRAS32186	1 1/4	1-4 (22pt)

AMERICAN STANDARD*
Lav/Kit/T&S Handle Pair
Chrome

Item #	Height (in)	Broach
ABRAS32188	29/32	1-4 (22pt)

AMERICAN STANDARD*
Diverter Handle
Chrome

Item #	Height (in)	Broach
ABRAS32188D	29/32	1-4 (22pt)

AMERICAN STANDARD*
Escutcheon
Chrome

Item #	O.D. (in)	I.D. (in)
ABRAS50329	3	1 3/8

AMERICAN STANDARD*
Escutcheon
Chrome

Item #	O.D. (in)	Height (in)	Thread
ABRAS50344	3	2	15/16-24

Quality Replacement Parts

AMERICAN STANDARD*
Escutcheon
Chrome

Item #	O.D. (in)	Height (in)	Thread
ABRAS50346	2 ½	1 $\frac{11}{16}$	$\frac{9}{16}$-20

AMERICAN STANDARD*
Escutcheon
Chrome

Item #	O.D. (in)	Height (in)	Thread
ABRAS50347	3	1 ½	$\frac{9}{16}$-20

AMERICAN STANDARD*
Tapped Escutcheon
Chrome

• For mating part see Fit-All ABRFA91620-S

Item #	O.D. (in)	Height (in)	Thread
ABRAS50348	3	1 ½	$\frac{9}{16}$-20

AMERICAN STANDARD*
Sleeve
Chrome
Colony
• For mating part see Fit-All ABRFA50320

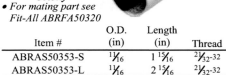

Item #	O.D. (in)	Length (in)	Thread
ABRAS50353-S	$\frac{11}{16}$	1 $\frac{15}{16}$	$\frac{21}{32}$-32
ABRAS50353-L	$\frac{11}{16}$	2 $\frac{15}{16}$	$\frac{21}{32}$-32

AMERICAN STANDARD*
Sleeve
Chrome

Item #	O.D. (in)	Length (in)	Thread
ABRAS50354	1 ⅜	1 ⅛	1.175 - 24

AMERICAN STANDARD*
Index Button
13/16" O.D.

Item #	H/C/D
ABRAS77103H	Hot
ABRAS77103C	Cold
ABRAS77103D	Diverter

AMERICAN STANDARD*
Index Button
5/8" O.D.

Item #	H/C	Color
ABRAS77104H	Hot	Red
ABRAS77104C	Cold	Blue

AMERICAN STANDARD*
Handle Nut
Chrome

Item #	H/C/D
ABRAS77179H	Hot
ABRAS77179C	Cold
ABRAS77179D	Diverter

AMERICAN STANDARD*
Seat
Rubber
Cadet

Item #
ABRAS9001

AMERICAN STANDARD*
Seat
Rubber
Aquaseal

Item #
ABRAS9002

BRIGGS*
Cartridge
Plastic

• Also for Bradley, Kohler & Sayco

Item #	Length
ABRBR10213	3 $\frac{11}{32}$

BRIGGS*
Gasket
Rubber

• Fits ABRBR10213

Item #
ABRBR10213-GASKET

BRIGGS*
Stem
Brass

• Includes gasket

Item #	Length (in)	Broach	H/C
ABRBR20251	4 ½	3-3 (18pt)	H or C

BRIGGS*
Stem
Brass

• Chrome Plated, includes gasket

Item #	Length (in)	Broach	H/C
ABRBR20252	5 ½	3-3 (18pt)	H or C

BRIGGS*
Cross Handle Pair
Chrome

• Also fits Indiana & Union Brass

Item #	Height (in)	Broach
ABRBR33246	$\frac{9}{16}$	3-3 (18pt)

To Order Call: 1.800.767.5552 . Fax: 1.800.886.9831

Original Mfg's names are used for identification only and are not a representation that the items offered are genuine items of the original Mfg.

BRIGGS*
Lav/Kit
Handle Pair
Chrome

- Also fits Indiana & Union Brass

Item #	Height (in)	Broach
ABRBR33651	29/32	3-3 (18pt)

BRIGGS*
Diverter
Handle
Chrome

- Also fits Indiana & Union Brass

Item #	Height (in)	Broach
ABRBR33651D	29/32	3-3 (18pt)

BRIGGS*
Lav/Kit
Handle
Acrylic

Item #	Height (in)	Broach
ABRBR404-07	2	

CENTRAL BRASS*
Stem
Brass
- Old Style
- Includes gasket

Item #	Length (in)	Broach	H/C
ABRCB10368-LF	1 17/32	1-6 (16pt)	Hot
ABRCB10369-LF	1 17/32	1-6 (16pt)	Cold

Send Your ABRASS Orders To:

BARRY E. WALTER SR. CO.

Fax or E-mail:
orderdesk@barrywalter.com

CENTRAL BRASS*
Stem
Brass
- New Style
- Includes gasket

NSF / ANSI 372 Compliant

Item #	Length (in)	Broach	H/C
ABRCB10370-LF	1 17/32	1-6 (16pt)	Hot
ABRCB10371-LF	1 17/32	1-6 (16pt)	Cold

CENTRAL BRASS*
Diverter Stem
Brass

- New Style, includes gasket

Item #	Length (in)	Broach
ABRCB20329	5 3/4	1-6 (16pt)

CENTRAL BRASS*
Stem
Brass

- Includes gasket

Item #	Length (in)	Broach	H/C
ABRCB20331	5 7/32	1-6 (16pt)	H or C

CENTRAL BRASS*
Stem
Brass

- Includes gasket

Item #	Length (in)	Broach	H/C
ABRCB20332	5 1/4	1-6 (16pt)	H or C

CENTRAL BRASS*
Stem
Brass

- Includes gasket

Item #	Length (in)	Broach	H/C
ABRCB20333	5	1-6 (16pt)	H or C

CENTRAL BRASS*
Stem
Brass

- Includes gasket

Item #	Size (in)	Broach	H/C
ABRCB20336	5.25	1-6 (16pt)	H or C

CENTRAL BRASS*
Stem
Brass

- Chrome plated stem and sleeve
- Includes gasket

Item #	Length (in)	Broach	H/C
ABRCB20337	5 1/4	1-6 (16pt)	H or C

CENTRAL BRASS*
Tub &
Shower
Handle Pair
Chrome

Item #	Height (in)	Broach
ABRCB32231	1 1/4	1-6 (16pt)

CENTRAL BRASS*
Diverter
Handle
Chrome

Item #	Height (in)	Broach
ABRCB32231D	1 1/4	1-6 (16pt)

CENTRAL BRASS*
Lavatory
Handle Pair
Chrome

Item #	Height (in)	Broach
ABRCB32232	1 1/16	1-6 (16pt)

To Order Call: 1.800.767.5552 . Fax: 1.800.886.9831

Original Mfg's names are used for identification only and are not a representation that the items offered are genuine items of the original Mfg.

5

Quality Replacement Parts

CENTRAL BRASS*
Tub & Shower Handle Pair
Chrome

Item #	Height (in)	Broach
ABRCB32233	1 1/8	1-6 (16pt)

CENTRAL BRASS*
Tub & Shower Handle Pair
Chrome

Item #	Height (in)	Broach
ABRCB32240	2 3/8	1-6 (16pt)

CENTRAL BRASS*
Diverter Handle
Chrome

Item #	Height (in)	Broach
ABRCB32240D	2 3/8	1-6 (16pt)

CENTRAL BRASS*
Lav/Kit Handle
Chrome

Item #	Height (in)	Broach	H/C
ABRCB32241H	1 1/8	1-6 (16pt)	Hot
ABRCB32241C	1 1/8	1-6 (16pt)	Cold
ABRCB32241	1 1/8	1-6 (16pt)	Pair

CENTRAL BRASS*
Handle Pair
Chrome

Item #	Height (in)	Broach
ABRCB33247	9/16	1-6 (16pt)

CENTRAL BRASS*
Escutcheon
Chrome

- For mating part see Fit-All ABRFA91620-S

Item #	O.D. (in)	Height (in)	Thread
ABRCB50421	2 3/4	2 1/4	9/16-20

CHG*
Stem Pair
Brass

NSF / ANSI 372 Compliant

- Includes chrome plated brass lock-nuts & gaskets
- Sold in pairs, fits Binford ABF3057 faucet

Item #
ABR3057-STEM-PR-LF

CHG*
Handle Pair
Chrome

- Fits Binford ABF3057 faucet

Item #
ABR3057-HDL-PR

CHICAGO*
Stem
Brass

- Chrome plated stem

Item #	Length (in)	Broach	H/C
ABRCH10320	2 1/16	3-12 (Sqr)	H
ABRCH10321	2 1/16	3-12 (Sqr)	C

CHICAGO*
Stem
Brass

NSF / ANSI 372 Compliant

- Chrome plated stem

Item #	Length (in)	Broach	H/C
ABRCH10320-LF	2 1/16	3-12 (Sqr)	H
ABRCH10321-LF	2 1/16	3-12 (Sqr)	C

CHICAGO*
Lav/Kit Handle Pair
Chrome
Quaturn

Item #	Height (in)	Broach
ABRCH32001	11/16	3-12 (Sqr)

CHICAGO*
ADA Lav/Kit Handle Pair
Chrome

Item #	Length (in)	Broach
ABRCH32002	4	3-12 (Sqr)

CHICAGO*
Index Ring
Plastic

Item #	Color	H/C
ABRCH77180H	Red	Hot
ABRCH77180C	Blue	Cold

CRANE*
Stem
Brass
Dial-EZE

NSF / ANSI 372 Compliant

- Includes gasket

Item #	Length (in)	Broach	H/C
ABRCR10312-LF	2 3/8	1-1 (12pt)	H
ABRCR10313-LF	2 3/8	1-1 (12pt)	C

CRANE*
Stem
Brass

Item #	Length (in)	Broach	H/C
ABRCR20334	4 21/32	2-5 (12pt)	H or C

Quality Replacement Parts

BRASS AMERICA
Quality Replacement Parts

CRANE*
Diverter Stem
Brass

- Includes gasket

Item #	Length (in)	Broach
ABRCR20341	4 19/32	2-5 (12pt)

CRANE*
Tub & Shower Handle Pair
Chrome

Item #	Height (in)	Broach
ABRCR32330	1 13/16	1-2 (12pt)

CRANE*
Diverter Handle
Chrome

Item #	Height (in)	Broach
ABRCR32330D	1 13/16	1-2 (12pt)

CRANE*
Tub & Shower Handle Pair
Chrome

Item #	Height (in)	Broach
ABRCR32335	1 3/4	1-1 (12pt)

CRANE*
Tub & Shower Handle Pair
Chrome

- Old Style

Item #	Height (in)	Broach
ABRCR32337	1 5/16	1-1 (12pt)

CRANE*
Tub & Shower Handle Pair
Chrome

- New Style

Item #	Height (in)	Broach
ABRCR32338	1 5/8	1-1 (12pt)

CRANE*
Lavatory Handle Pair
Chrome

- New Style

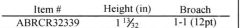

Item #	Height (in)	Broach
ABRCR32339	1 13/32	1-1 (12pt)

CRANE*
Tub & Shower Handle Pair
Chrome

- New Style

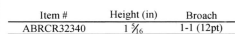

Item #	Height (in)	Broach
ABRCR32340	1 5/16	1-1 (12pt)

CRANE*
Index Button
1 3/32" O.D.
32335

Item #	H/C/D
ABRCR77121H	Hot
ABRCR77121C	Cold
ABRCR77121D	Diverter

DELTA*
Push/Pull Diverter Cartridge
Brass

- Chrome plated stem

Item #	Length (in)
ABRDE10420	3 25/32

DELTA*
Cartridge
Plastic

- Brass Post & S.S. Base
- Also Fits: Jameco, Price Pfister & Glacier Bay

Item #	Broach	H/C
ABRDE10421	D	H or C

DELTA*
Cartridge
Plastic

Item #	Length (in)	Broach	H/C
ABRDE10422	1 15/16	D	H or C

DELTA*
Cartridge
Plastic

- Brass Post & S.S. Base

Item #	Length (in)	Broach	H/C
ABRDE10423	1 7/8	D	H or C

DELTA*
Cartridge
Plastic

- Plastic Post & S.S. Base

Item #	Length (in)	Broach	H/C
ABRDE10424	1 7/8	D	H or C

DELTA*
Stem Extender
Plastic

- Brass post

Item #	Length (in)	Broach
ABRDE10426	3	D

To Order Call: 1.800.767.5552 . Fax: 1.800.886.9831

Original Mfg's names are used for identification only and are not a representation that the items offered are genuine items of the original Mfg.

DELTA*
Scald Guard Escutcheon
Chrome

Item #
ABRDE50317

DELTA*
Stem Extender
Plastic

Item #	Length (in)	Broach
ABRDE5200EX	3	D

DELTA*
ADA Handle Pair
Chrome

- 4" Blades
- For Hospital Use

Item #	Length (in)	Broach
ABRDE33961	4	D

DELTA*
Lav/Kit Handle
Acrylic

- Includes Hex adapter & uses #70 ball

Item #	Height (in)
ABRDE404-01WA	2 ¼

DELTA*
Lav/Kit Handle
Acrylic

- Uses #212 ball

Item #	Height (in)
ABRDE404-02	2 ¼

DELTA*
Tub & Shower Handle
Acrylic

- #212 Offset
- Single Lever

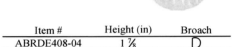

Item #	Height (in)
ABRDE404-03	2 ¼

DELTA*
Lav/Kit Handle Pair
Acrylic
Old Style

Item #	Height (in)	Broach
ABRDE408-04	1 ⅞	D

DELTA*
Lav/Kit Handle Pair
Acrylic

- For widespread lavatory

Item #	Height (in)	Broach
ABRDE408-16	2 ⅛	D

DELTA*
Index Button
1 1/4" O.D.

- Fits Binford faucet ABF5510
- For use in handle model ABRDE404-01WA

Item #
ABRDE7404-01

DELTA*
Index Button
23/32" O.D.

Item #	H/C
ABRDLX-INDEX-H	Hot
ABRDLX-INDEX-C	Cold

✓ NSF / ANSI 372
Compliant

DELTA*
#70 Ball
Stainless Steel

- Single Lever
- Lavatory only

Item #	Broach
ABRDE1-70SS	Round

✓ NSF / ANSI 372
Compliant

DELTA*
#70 Ball
Stainless Steel

- Single Lever
- For Lav/T&S
- OEM style with fourth hole

Item #	Broach
ABRDE1-70SS-OEM	Round

DELTA*
#70 Ball
Brass

- Single Lever

Item #	Broach
ABRDE1-70B	Round

✓ NSF / ANSI 372
Compliant

DELTA*
#70 Ball
Brass

- Single Lever

Item #	Broach
ABRDE1-70B-LF	Round

DELTA*
#70 Ball
Brass

- Single Lever
- High Volume

Item #	Broach
ABRDE1-70B-SP	Round

DELTA*
#212 Ball
Brass

• Single Lever

Item #	Broach
ABRDE1-212B	Diamond

NSF / ANSI 372 Compliant

DELTA*
#212 Ball
Brass

• Single Lever

Item #	Broach
ABRDE1-212B-LF	Diamond

NSF / ANSI 372 Compliant

DELTA*
#212 Ball
Stainless Steel

• Single Lever

Item #	Broach
ABRDE1-212SS	Diamond

DELTA*
Repair Kit
Single Lever

• Includes: Cam assembly, seats, springs and S.S. Ball (#70)

Item #
ABRDE-KIT-1

DELTA*
Repair Kit
Seats/Springs

• Includes: two each, new style seats and springs

Item #
ABRDE-KIT-2

ELJER*
Stem
Brass

• For mating part see Fit-All ABRFA50322
• Includes gasket

Item #	Length (in)	Broach	H/C
ABREL20524	4 19/32	1-6 (16pt)	H or C

ELJER*
Diverter Stem
Brass

• For mating part see Fit-All ABRFA50322
• Includes gasket

Item #	Length (in)	Broach
ABREL20525	4 29/32	1-6 (16pt)

ELJER*
Stem
Brass

• For mating part see Fit-All ABRFA50322
• Includes sleeve & gasket

Item #	Length (in)	Broach	H/C
ABREL20526	4 19/32	1-6 (16pt)	H
ABREL20533	4 19/32	1-6 (16pt)	C

ELJER*
Diverter Stem
Brass

• For mating part see Fit-All ABRFA50322
• Includes sleeve & gasket

Item #	Length (in)	Broach
ABREL20527	4 23/32	1-6 (16pt)

ELJER*
Stem
Brass

• For mating part see Fit-All ABRFA50322
• Includes sleeve & gasket

Item #	Length (in)	Broach	H/C
ABREL20528	4 7/32	1-6 (16pt)	H or C

ELJER*
Diverter Stem
Brass

• For mating part see Fit-All ABRFA50322
• Includes sleeve & gasket

Item #	Length (in)	Broach
ABREL20529	4 15/64	1-6 (16pt)

ELJER*
ADA Handle Pair
Chrome

Item #	Length (in)	Broach
ABREL33151	4	1-6 (16pt)

ELJER*
Tub & Shower Handle Pair
Chrome

Item #	Height (in)	Broach
ABREL33152	1 1/8	1-6 (16pt)

ELJER*
Diverter Handle
Chrome

Item #	Height (in)	Broach
ABREL33152D	1 1/8	1-6 (16pt)

ELJER*
Lavatory Handle Pair
Chrome

Item #	Height (in)	Broach
ABREL33613	1 3/16	1-6 (16pt)

ELJER*
Lavatory Handle Pair
Chrome

Item #	Height (in)	Broach
ABREL33614	$^{15}/_{16}$	1-6 (16pt)

ELJER*
Lavatory Handle Pair
Chrome
Lustra

Item #	Height (in)	Broach
ABREL33815	$1^{1}/_{16}$	1-6 (16pt)

ELJER*
Tub & Shower Handle Pair
Chrome
Lustra

Item #	Height (in)	Broach
ABREL33820	$1^{1}/_{8}$	1-6 (16pt)

ELJER*
Diverter Handle
Chrome
Lustra

Item #	Height (in)	Broach
ABREL33820D	$1^{1}/_{8}$	1-6 (16pt)

FEBCO*
Bonnet & Poppet Assembly
Plastic

- Fits Febco #765 vacuum breaker
- *Febco is a registered trade name and is not affiliated or associated with Abrass America or the Barry E. Walter Sr. Company*

Item #	Size (in)	Febco Cross Ref.
ABRFEB182512	$^{3}/_{4}$	905-211

FEBCO*
Bonnet & Poppet Assembly
Plastic

- Fits Febco #765 vacuum breaker
- *Febco is a registered trade name and is not affiliated or associated with Abrass America or the Barry E. Walter Sr. Company*

Item #	Size (in)	Febco Cross Ref.
ABRFEB091011	1	905-212

FEBCO*
Gasket Repair Kit
Plastic

- Fits 1" bonnet & poppet assembly

Item #	Size (in)
ABRFEB19A	1

FEBCO*
Gasket Repair Kit
Plastic

- Fits 3/4" bonnet & poppet assembly

Item #	Size (in)
ABRFEB19B	$2^{3}/_{8}$

FIT-ALL
Tub & Shower Handle Pair
Chrome

- Pair is packaged with two universal adapters
- Will accept brass handle spud

Item #	Height (in)
ABRFA32235	$1^{1}/_{8}$

FIT-ALL
Tub & Shower Handle Pair
Chrome

- Pair is packaged with two universal adapters
- Will accept brass handle spud

Item #	Height (in)
ABRFA32245	1

FIT-ALL
ADA Handle Pair
Chrome

- Pair is packaged with two universal adapters
- Will accept brass handle spud

Item #	Length (in)
ABRFA32255	$2^{1}/_{4}$

FIT-ALL
Handle Pair
Porcelain

- Pair is packaged with a variety of adaptors, screws and spacers
- Will accept brass handle spud

Item #	Height (in)
ABRFA32266	$2^{3}/_{8}$

FIT-ALL
Handle Pair
Chrome

- Pair is packaged with a variety of adaptors, screws and spacers
- Will accept brass handle spud

Item #	Height (in)
ABRFA32267CP	$2^{3}/_{8}$

FIT-ALL
Handle Pair
Polished Brass

- Pair is packaged with a variety of adaptors, screws and spacers
- Will accept brass handle spud

Item #	Height (in)
ABRFA32267PB	$2^{3}/_{8}$

Send Your ABRASS Orders To:

BARRY E. WALTER SR. CO.

Fax or E-mail:
orderdesk@barrywalter.com

Original Mfg's names are used for identification only and are not a representation that the items offered are genuine items of the original Mfg.

FIT-ALL
Handle Pair
Chrome

- *Pair is packaged with a variety of adaptors, screws and spacers*
- *Will accept brass handle spud*

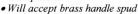

Item #	Height (in)
ABRFA32270	2 ⅜

FIT-ALL
Handle Pair
Porcelain

- *Pair is packaged with a variety of adaptors, screws and spacers*
- *Will accept brass handle spud*

Item #	Height (in)
ABRFA32271	2 ⅜

FIT-ALL
Tub & Shower Handle Pair
Chrome

- *Pair is packaged with two universal adapters*
- *Will accept brass handle spud*

Item #	Length (in)
ABRFA32410	5

FIT-ALL
Lav/Kit Handle Pair
Chrome

- *Pair is packaged with two universal adapters*
- *Will accept brass handle spud*

Item #	Height (in)
ABRFA32411	1 ⅜

FIT-ALL
Tub & Shower Handle Pair
Chrome

- *Pair is packaged with two universal adapters*
- *Will accept brass handle spud*

Item #	Height (in)
ABRFA32412	1 ½

FIT-ALL
Tub & Shower Handle Pair
Chrome

- *Pair is packaged with two universal adapters*
- *Will accept brass handle spud*

Item #	Height (in)
ABRFA32451	1 ¼

FIT-ALL
Tub & Shower Handle Pair
Chrome

- *Pair is packaged with two universal adapters*
- *Will accept brass handle spud*

Item #	Height (in)
ABRFA32452	1 ½

FIT-ALL
Tub & Shower Handle Pair
Chrome

- *Pair is packaged with two universal adapters*
- *Will accept brass handle spud*

Item #	Height (in)
ABRFA32453	1 ¾

FIT-ALL
Tub & Shower Handle Pair
Acrylic

- *Pair is packaged with two universal adapters*
- *Will accept brass handle spud*

Item #	Height (in)
ABRFA32480	1 ¾

FIT-ALL
Tub & Shower Handle Pair
Chrome

- *Pair is packaged with two universal adapters*
- *Will accept brass handle spud*

Item #	Height (in)
ABRFA32801	2 ½

FIT-ALL
Lav/Kit Handle Pair
Chrome

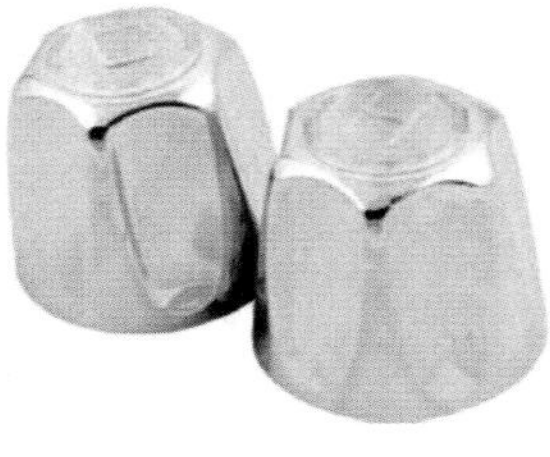

- *Pair is packaged with two universal adapters*
- *Will accept brass handle spud*

Item #	Height (in)
ABRFA32802	1 ⅝

FIT-ALL
Tub & Shower Handle Pair
Chrome
Vise-Grip

Item #	Height (in)
ABRFA33720	1 ⅛

FIT-ALL
Tub & Shower Handle Pair
Chrome
Vise-Grip

Item #	Height (in)
ABRFA33740	1 ⅛

FIT-ALL
Tub & Shower Handle Pair
Acrylic
Vise-Grip

Item #	Height (in)
ABRFA33780	2

Send Your ABRASS Orders To:

BARRY E. WALTER SR. CO.

Fax or E-mail:
orderdesk@barrywalter.com

To Order Call: 1.800.767.5552 . Fax: 1.800.886.9831

*Original Mfg's names are used for identification only and are not a representation that the items offered are genuine items of the original Mfg.   *11*

Quality Replacement Parts

Quality Replacement Parts

FIT-ALL
Tub & Shower Handle Pair
Acrylic

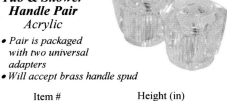

- Pair is packaged with two universal adapters
- Will accept brass handle spud

Item #	Height (in)
ABRFA408-10	2

FIT-ALL
Tub & Shower Handle Pair
Acrylic

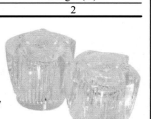

- Pair is packaged with two universal adapters
- Will accept brass handle spud

Item #	Height (in)	Broach
ABRFA408-10L	2 $\frac{5}{8}$	Long

FIT-ALL
Tub & Shower Handle Pair
Acrylic

- Pair is packaged with two universal adapters
- Will accept brass handle spud

Item #	Height (in)	Broach
ABRFA408-10S	2 $\frac{5}{8}$	Short

FIT-ALL
Escutcheon
Chrome

- Set screw included

Item #	O.D. (in)	I.D. (in)
ABRFA50318	2 $\frac{1}{16}$	1 $\frac{5}{16}$

FIT-ALL
Escutcheon
Chrome
Fits American Standard

- Set screw included

Item #	O.D. (in)	I.D. (in)
ABRFA50320	2 $\frac{1}{16}$	1 $\frac{1}{16}$

FIT-ALL
Escutcheon
Chrome
Fits American Standard, Nibco

- Set screw included

Item #	O.D. (in)	I.D. (in)
ABRFA50321	2 $\frac{1}{16}$	$\frac{13}{16}$

FIT-ALL
Escutcheon
Chrome
Fits Eljer, Sterling, Indiana & Milwaukee

- Set screw included

Item #	O.D. (in)	I.D. (in)
ABRFA50322	2 $\frac{1}{16}$	1

FIT-ALL
Escutcheon
Chrome

- Set screw included

Item #	O.D. (in)	I.D. (in)
ABRFA50323	2 $\frac{1}{16}$	1 $\frac{1}{8}$

FIT-ALL
Escutcheon
Chrome

- Set screw included

Item #	O.D. (in)	I.D. (in)
ABRFA50324	2 $\frac{1}{16}$	1 $\frac{1}{4}$

FIT-ALL
Escutcheon
Chrome
Fits Gerber, Briggs & Kohler

- Set screw included

Item #	O.D. (in)	I.D. (in)
ABRFA50325	2 $\frac{3}{4}$	1 $\frac{1}{8}$

FIT-ALL
Escutcheon
Chrome
Fits Price Pfister, Central, Sayco, Sterling & Streamway

- Set screw included

Item #	O.D. (in)	I.D. (in)
ABRFA50326	2 $\frac{3}{4}$	1 $\frac{1}{4}$

FIT-ALL
Escutcheon
Chrome
Fits Crane

- Set screw included

Item #	O.D. (in)	I.D. (in)
ABRFA50327	2 $\frac{3}{4}$	1 $\frac{3}{8}$

FIT-ALL
Escutcheon
Chrome
Fits Savoy

- Set screw included

Item #	O.D. (in)	I.D. (in)
ABRFA50330	2 $\frac{1}{16}$	1 $\frac{1}{16}$

FIT-ALL
Escutcheon
Chrome

- Reversible
- See ABRFA50332 & ABRFA50353 for mating part

Item #	Length (in)	Width (in)	Height (in)
ABRFA50331	4 $\frac{1}{16}$	2 $\frac{3}{4}$	1 $\frac{9}{16}$

Send Your ABRASS Orders To:

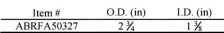

BARRY E. 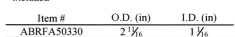 SR. CO.

Fax or E-mail:
orderdesk@barrywalter.com

To Order Call: 1.800.767.5552 . Fax: 1.800.886.9831

Original Mfg's names are used for identification only and are not a representation that the items offered are genuine items of the original Mfg.

BRASS AMERICA
Quality Replacement Parts

FIT-ALL
Escutcheon
Chrome

Item #	O.D. (in)	Height (in)	Thread
ABRFA50341-24T	2 7/8	1 3/4	5/8-24

FIT-ALL
Escutcheon
Chrome

Item #	O.D. (in)	Height (in)	I.D. (in)
ABRFA50350	2 13/16	1 3/4	5/8

FIT-ALL
Escutcheon
Chrome
- Reversible
- See ABRFA50332 & ABRFA50353 for mating part

Item #	O.D. (in)	Height (in)
ABRFA50351	2 3/4	1 9/16

FIT-ALL
Escutcheon
Chrome

Item #	O.D. (in)	Height (in)	Thread
ABRFA50361	2 3/4	1 9/16	5/8-24
ABRFA50361-18T	2 3/4	1 9/16	5/8-18

FIT-ALL
Escutcheon
Chrome

Item #	O.D. (in)	Height (in)	I.D. (in)
ABRFA50372	2 13/16	1 3/4	9/16

FIT-ALL
Escutcheon
Chrome

Item #	O.D. (in)	Height (in)	I.D. (in)
ABRFA50380	2 13/16	1 3/4	3/4

FIT-ALL
Sleeve
Chrome
- Reversible

Item #	O.D. (in)	Height (in)	Thread
ABRFA50332	1 1/4	1 1/16	5/8-18

FIT-ALL
Sleeve
Chrome
- Reversible

Item #	O.D. (in)	Height (in)	Thread
ABRFA50352	1 1/4	1 1/16	5/8-24

FIT-ALL
Tapered Nipple
Plastic

Item #	Length (in)	TPI
ABRFA50362	3 1/4	Various

FIT-ALL
Tapered Nipple
Plastic

Item #	Length (in)	TPI
ABRFA50363	2	21/32-18

FIT-ALL
Index Button
5/8" O.D.
Fits American Standard

Item #	H/C/D
ABRFA77101H	Hot
ABRFA77101C	Cold
ABRFA77101D	Diverter

FIT-ALL
Index Button
3/4" O.D.
Fits American Standard

Item #	H/C/D
ABRFA77102H	Hot
ABRFA77102C	Cold
ABRFA77102D	Diverter

FIT-ALL
Index Button
1 1/4" O.D.

Item #	H/C/D
ABRFA77112H	Hot
ABRFA77112C	Cold
ABRFA77112D	Diverter

FIT-ALL
Index Button
3/4" O.D.

Item #	H/C/D
ABRFA77116H	Hot
ABRFA77116C	Cold
ABRFA77116D	Diverter

Original Mfg's names are used for identification only and are not a representation that the items offered are genuine items of the original Mfg.

FIT-ALL
Index Button
1/2" O.D.
Chrome

Item #	H/C/D
ABRFA77161H	Hot
ABRFA77161C	Cold
ABRFA77161D	Diverter

FIT-ALL
Index Button
1/2" O.D.
Polished Brass

Item #	H/C/D
ABRFA77161H-PB	Hot
ABRFA77161C-PB	Cold
ABRFA77161D-PB	Diverter

FIT-ALL
Escutcheon Nipple
Brass

- Fits American Standard & Central

Item #	Length (in)	TPI
ABRFA91620-L	5	9/16-20

FIT-ALL
Escutcheon Nipple
Brass

- Fits American Standard & Central

Item #	Length (in)	TPI
ABRFA91620-S	2 1/2	9/16-20

FIT-ALL
Escutcheon Nipple
Brass

- Fits Briggs, Gerber, Indiana Brass & Union Brass

Item #	Length (in)	TPI
ABRFA5824S	2 1/2	5/8-24

FISHER*
Lav/Kit Handle
Chrome

Item #	Length (in)	Broach	H/C
ABRFI32601H	2	3-31(12pt)	Hot
ABRFI32601C	2	3-31(12pt)	Cold
ABRFI32601	2	3-31(12pt)	Pair

 NSF / ANSI 372 Compliant

GERBER*
Stem
Brass
New Style

- Includes gasket

Item #	Length (in)	Broach	H/C
ABRGE10724-LF	1 5/8	2-3 (16pt)	H
ABRGE10725-LF	1 5/8	2-3 (16pt)	C

NSF / ANSI 372 Compliant

GERBER*
Cartridge
Plastic

- Includes gasket

Item #	Length (in)	Broach	H/C
ABRGE10726-LF	1 23/32	2-3 (16pt)	H
ABRGE10727-LF	1 23/32	2-3 (16pt)	C

GERBER*
Stem
Brass

- Includes gasket

Item #	Length (in)	Broach	H/C
ABRGE20778B	5 1/4	2-3 (16pt)	H or C

GERBER*
Diverter Stem
Brass

- Includes gasket

Item #	Length (in)	Broach
ABRGE20779	5 3/4	2-3 (16pt)

GERBER*
Tub & Shower Handle Pair
Chrome

Item #	Height (in)	Broach
ABRGE32500	2 1/2	2-3 (16pt) Long

GERBER*
Diverter Handle
Chrome

Item #	Height (in)	Broach
ABRGE32500D	2 1/2	2-3 (16pt) Long

GERBER*
Tub & Shower Handle Pair
Chrome

Item #	Height (in)	Broach
ABRGE32501	2 1/2	2-3 (16pt) Short

GERBER*
Diverter Handle
Chrome

Item #	Height (in)	Broach
ABRGE32501D	2 1/2	2-3 (16pt) Short

GERBER*
Lav/Kit Handle Pair
Chrome

Item #	Height (in)	Broach
ABRGE32510	1 1/2	2-3 (16pt)

To Order Call: 1.800.767.5552 . Fax: 1.800.886.9831

14   *Original Mfg's names are used for identification only and are not a representation that the items offered are genuine items of the original Mfg.*

Quality Replacement Parts

BRASS AMERICA
Quality Replacement Parts

GERBER*
ADA Lav/Kit Handle Pair
Chrome

Item #	Length (in)	Broach
ABRGE32511	4	2-3 (16pt)

GERBER*
Lav/Kit Handle Pair
Chrome

Item #	Height (in)	Broach
ABRGE32520	1 1/16	2-3 (16pt)

GERBER*
Diverter Handle
Chrome

Item #	Height (in)	Broach
ABRGE32521D	1 1/16	2-3 (16pt)

GERBER*
Tub & Shower Handle Pair
Chrome

Item #	Height (in)	Broach
ABRGE32540	1	2-3 (16pt)

GERBER*
Handle Pair
Chrome

• *Also fits Sayco*

Item #	Height (in)	Broach
ABRGE32541	3/4	2-3 (16pt)

GERBER*
Diverter Handle
Chrome

• *Also fits Sayco*

Item #	Height (in)	Broach
ABRGE32541D	3/4	2-3 (16pt)

GERBER*
Escutcheon
Chrome

Item #	Length (in)	Width (in)	I.D. (in)
ABRGE50377	4 1/4	2 3/4	1 1/8

GERBER*
Escutcheon
Chrome

• *See ABRFA5824S for mating part*

Item #	O.D. (in)	Height (in)	Thread
ABRGE50403	2 3/4	2 1/2	9/16-24

GERBER*
Sleeve
Chrome

• *See ABRFA50325 for mating part*

Item #	O.D. (in)	Length (in)	Thread
ABRGE50437	1 1/8	3 3/4	1 1/16-32

GERBER*
Index Button
1 1/16" O.D.

Item #	H/C/D
ABRGE77122H	Hot
ABRGE77122C	Cold
ABRGE77122D	Diverter

HARCRAFT*
Stem
Brass

• *Includes gasket*

Item #	Size (in)	Broach	H/C
ABRHA20831	4 1/2	1-2 (12pt)	H or C

HARCRAFT*
Diverter Stem
Brass

Item #	Size (in)	Broach
ABRHA20834	4 1/4	1-2 (12pt)

HARCRAFT*
Tub & Shower Handle Pair
Chrome

Item #	Height (in)	Broach
ABRHA32646	2 5/8	1-2 (12pt)

HARCRAFT*
Diverter Handle
Chrome

Item #	Height (in)	Broach
ABRHA32646D	2 5/8	1-2 (12pt)

HARCRAFT*
Lavatory Handle Pair
Chrome

Item #	Height (in)	Broach
ABRHA32647	1 3/4	1-2 (12pt)

To Order Call: 1.800.767.5552 . Fax: 1.800.886.9831

Quality Replacement Parts

HARCRAFT*
Escutcheon
Chrome

Item #	O.D. (in)	Height (in)	Thread
ABRHA50340	2 7/8	2 5/8	7/8-20

HARCRAFT*
Index Button
1 11/16" O.D.

Item #	H/C
ABRHA77176H	Hot
ABRHA77176C	Cold

HARCRAFT*
Index Button
2" O.D.

Item #	H/C/D
ABRHA77177H	Hot
ABRHA77177C	Cold
ABRHA77177D	Diverter

INDIANA BRASS*
Stem
Brass

Item #	Length (in)	Broach	H/C
ABRIN20911	3 9/16	3-3 (18pt)	H
ABRIN20912	3 9/16	3-3 (18pt)	C

INDIANA BRASS*
Lav/Kit Handle Pair
Chrome
- *Also fits Briggs & Union Brass*

Item #	Height (in)	Broach
ABRIN33610	7/8	3-3 (18pt)

INDIANA BRASS*
Tub & Shower Handle Pair
Chrome
- *Also fits Briggs & Union Brass*

Item #	Height (in)	Broach
ABRIN33611	1 3/16	3-3 (18pt)

INDIANA BRASS*
Tub & Shower Handle Pair
Chrome
- *Also fits Briggs & Union Brass*

Item #	Height (in)	Broach
ABRIN33615	1 1/8	3-3 (18pt)

INDIANA BRASS*
Diverter Handle
Chrome
- *Also fits Briggs & Union Brass*

Item #	Height (in)	Broach
ABRIN33615D	1 1/8	3-3 (18pt)

INDIANA BRASS*
Sleeve
Chrome
- *See ABRFA50322 for mating part*

Item #	O.D. (in)	Length (in)	Thread
ABRIN50384	1	2 5/16	3 1/32-32

KOHLER*
Stem
Ceramic
- *Nickel Plated Brass*

Item #	Size (in)	Broach	H/C
ABRKO11101-LF	2 7/32	1-7 (19pt)	H
ABRKO11102-LF	2 7/32	1-7 (19pt)	C

KOHLER*
Stem
Brass
- *Chrome Plated Stem*
- *Brass Plunger*

Item #	Size (in)	Broach	H/C
ABRKO11124-LF	2 1/2	1-7 (19pt)	H
ABRKO11125-LF	2 1/2	1-7 (19pt)	C

KOHLER*
Barrel
Brass

Item #	Length (in)	H/C
ABRKO11126-LF	1 3/8	Hot or Cold

KOHLER*
Stem
Brass
Trend
- *Nickel Plated Gland*
- *Includes gasket*

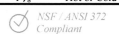

Item #	Size (in)	Broach	H/C
ABRKO11127-LF	1 15/32	1-6 (16pt)	H
ABRKO11128-LF	1 15/32	1-6 (16pt)	C

KOHLER*
Stem
Brass
Valvet
- *Chrome Plated Stem*
- *Plastic Plunger*

Item #	Size (in)	Broach	H/C
ABRKO11134	2 1/2	1-7 (19pt)	H
ABRKO11135	2 1/2	1-7 (19pt)	C

KOHLER*
Stem
Brass
Valvet
- *Chrome Plated Stem*
- *Plastic Plunger*

Item #	Size (in)	Broach	H/C
ABRKO11134-LF	2 1/2	1-7 (19pt)	H
ABRKO11135-LF	2 1/2	1-7 (19pt)	C

To Order Call: 1.800.767.5552 . Fax: 1.800.886.9831

16   *Original Mfg's names are used for identification only and are not a representation that the items offered are genuine items of the original Mfg.*

BRASS AMERICA
Quality Replacement Parts

NSF / ANSI 372 Compliant

KOHLER*
Cartridge
Plastic
Coralais

Item #	Length (in)	Broach	H/C
ABRKO11158	1 15/32	D	H
ABRKO11159	1 15/32	D	C

KOHLER*
Stem
Brass
Trend
• *Includes nipple*

Item #	Length (in)	Broach	H/C
ABRKO21101	4 1/4	1-6 (16pt)	H or C

KOHLER*
Stem
Brass
Shoreham Trend
• *Includes sleeve*

Item #	Length (in)	Broach	H/C
ABRKO21102	4 1/4	1-6 (16pt)	H
ABRKO21103	4 1/4	1-6 (16pt)	C

KOHLER*
Stem
Brass
O.S. Dalney

• *Chrome Plated Stem, includes gasket*

Item #	Length (in)	Broach	H/C
ABRKO21104	6 1/8	1-7 (19pt)	H or C

KOHLER*
Diverter Stem
Brass
Trend
• *Includes nipple*

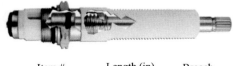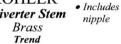

Item #	Length (in)	Broach
ABRKO21111	5	1-6 (16pt)

KOHLER*
Diverter Stem
Brass
Trend
• *Includes nipple*

Item #	Length (in)	Broach
ABRKO21112	5 1/4	1-6 (16pt)

KOHLER*
Diverter Stem
Brass
Valvet
• *Chrome Plated Stem*

Item #	Length (in)	Broach
ABRKO21113	5 1/8	1-7 (19pt)

KOHLER*
Diverter Stem
Brass
Shoreham Trend

Item #	Length (in)
ABRKO21114	5 1/4

KOHLER*
Diverter Stem
Brass
Shoreham Trend
• *Includes sleeve*

Item #	Length (in)
ABRKO21115	5 13/32

KOHLER*
Lav/Kit Handle Pair
Chrome
Triton

Item #	Height (in)	Broach
ABRKO32630	1 1/2	1-7 (19pt)

KOHLER*
Lav/Kit Handle Pair
Chrome
Constellation/ Triton II

Item #	Height (in)	Broach
ABRKO32631	1 3/8	1-7 (19pt)

KOHLER*
Tub & Shower Handle Pair
Chrome
Constellation/ Triton II

Item #	Height (in)	Broach
ABRKO32632	1 3/4	1-7 (19pt)

KOHLER*
Diverter Handle
Chrome
Constellation/ Triton II

Item #	Height (in)	Broach
ABRKO32632D	1 3/4	1-7 (19pt)

KOHLER*
Tub & Shower Handle Pair
Chrome
Triton

Item #	Height (in)	Broach
ABRKO32635	1 9/16	1-7 (19pt)

KOHLER*
Tub & Shower Handle Pair
Chrome
Triton

Item #	Height (in)	Broach
ABRKO32636	2	1-7 (19pt)

*Original Mfg's names are used for identification only and are not a representation that the items offered are genuine items of the original Mfg.

KOHLER*
Lav/Kit Handle Pair
Chrome
Trend

Item #	Height (in)	Broach
ABRKO32640	1 ¾	1-6 (16pt)

KOHLER*
Tub & Shower Handle Pair
Chrome
Trend

Item #	Height (in)	Broach
ABRKO32641	2	1-6 (16pt)

KOHLER*
Diverter Handle
Chrome
Trend

Item #	Height (in)	Broach
ABRKO32641D	2	1-6 (16pt)

KOHLER*
Lav/Kit Handle Pair
Acrylic
Trend

• With ABS

Item #	Height (in)	Broach
ABRKO408-13	1 ¾	1-6 (16pt)

KOHLER*
Nipple
Plastic

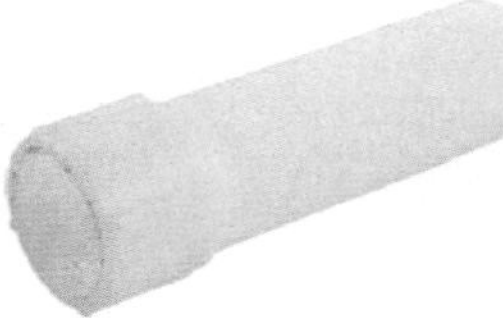

Item #	Length (in)	Thread
ABRKO50366S	2 ½	¾-16

KOHLER*
Escutcheon
Chrome

Item #	O.D. (in)	I.D. (in)
ABRKO50373	2 ½	¾

KOHLER*
Escutcheon
Chrome

Item #	O.D. (in)	Height (in)	Thread
ABRKO50381	2 ½	1 ¼	1 ⁵⁄₁₆-16

KOHLER*
Escutcheon
Chrome
Trend

Item #	O.D. (in)	Height (in)	Thread
ABRKO50422	2 ¾	2 ¼	¾-16

KOHLER*
Index Button
13/16" O.D.

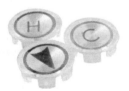

Item #	H/C/D	Color
ABRKO77131H	Hot	Red
ABRKO77131C	Cold	Blue
ABRKO77131D	Diverter	Black

KOHLER*
Index Button
9/16" O.D.

• For ADA handle

Item #	H/C/D	Color
ABRKO77132H	Hot	Red
ABRKO77132C	Cold	Blue

MILWAUKEE*
Cartridge
Plastic

Item #	Length (in)	Broach	H/C
ABRMW11323	1 ⁷⁄₃₂		Hot

MILWAUKEE*
Cartridge
Plastic

Item #	Length (in)	Broach	H/C
ABRMW11324	1 ⁷⁄₃₂		Cold

MILWAUKEE*
Cartridge
Plastic

Item #	Length (in)	Broach	H/C
ABRMW11325	1 ½		H or C

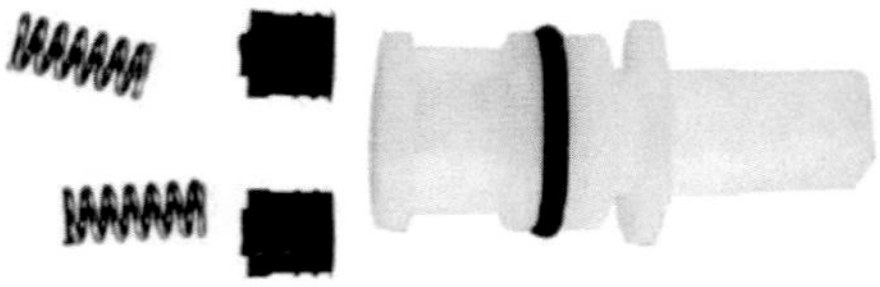

MILWAUKEE*
Cartridge
Plastic

Item #	Length (in)	Broach	H/C
ABRMW11326	2		H or C

MILWAUKEE*
Cartridge
Plastic

Item #	Length (in)	Broach	H/C
ABRMW11327	2 ⅛		H or C

To Order Call: 1.800.767.5552 . Fax: 1.800.886.9831

18   *Original Mfg's names are used for identification only and are not a representation that the items offered are genuine items of the original Mfg.*

Quality Replacement Parts

MILWAUKEE*
Stem
Brass

- *With copper gasket*

Item #	Length (in)	Broach	H/C
ABRMW21323	4 15/32	16pt	H or C

MIXET*
Single Lever Cartridge
Brass

- *Includes sleeve*

Item #	Length (in)	H/C
ABRMX21348-B	4 1/2	H or C

MIXET*
Tub & Shower Handle
Acrylic

Item #	Height (in)	Color
ABRMX404-16S	1	Smoke
ABRMX404-16C	1	Clear

MIXET*
Tub & Shower Handle
Chrome

- *Lever Style*

Item #	Length (in)
ABRMX404-17	3 7/8

MIXET*
Tub & Shower Handle
Acrylic

- *Short lever style*

Item #	Length (in)
ABRMX404-18	2 1/4

MIXET*
Loop Handle
Chrome

- *Fits ABRMX21348*
- *Remove insert to fit most single lever cartridges with square broaches*

Item #
ABRMX34103

MIXET*
Escutcheon
Chrome

Item #	O.D. (in)	I.D. (in)
ABRMX50337	5 1/2	1 1/4

MOEN*
Cartridge
Plastic
Hi Flo

Item #	Length (in)	Broach
ABRMO11300	2 5/8	

MOEN*
Cartridge
Plastic

Item #	Length (in)	Broach	H/C
ABRMO11301	2 5/8		H or C

MOEN*
Single Lever Cartridge
Plastic
- *Brass Core*

Item #	Length (in)	Broach
ABRMO21304	3 15/16	◯

MOEN*
Single Lever Cartridge
Plastic

NSF / ANSI 372 Compliant

- *Brass Core*

Item #	Length (in)	Broach
ABRMO21304-LF	3 15/16	◯

MOEN*
Single Lever Cartridge
Brass

Item #	Length (in)	Broach
ABRMO21305	3 15/16	◯

MOEN*
Single Lever Cartridge
Brass

NSF / ANSI 372 Compliant

Item #	Length (in)	Broach
ABRMO21305-LF	3 15/16	◯

MOEN*
Single Lever Cartridge
Plastic
Posi Temp
- *Pressure balance*

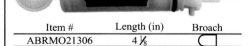

Item #	Length (in)	Broach
ABRMO21306	4 1/8	

MOEN*
Diverter Handle
Chrome
Posi Temp

- *Index included*

Item #	Height (in)	Broach
ABRMO32701	1 1/4	◯

To Order Call: 1.800.767.5552 . Fax: 1.800.886.9831

Original Mfg's names are used for identification only and are not a representation that the items offered are genuine items of the original Mfg.   19

Quality Replacement Parts

MOEN*
Tub & Shower Handle
Acrylic
Boutique Legend

• For single handle faucet

Item #	Height (in)	Broach
ABRMO404-10L	1 ¾	◻ (long)

MOEN*
Lavatory Handle
Acrylic
Boutique Legend

• For single handle faucet

Item #	Height (in)	Broach
ABRMO404-10S	1 ¾	◻ (short)

MOEN*
Tub & Shower Handle
Acrylic
Chateau New Style

• For single handle faucet

Item #	Height (in)	Broach
ABRMO404-12L	1 ⅝	◻ (long)

MOEN*
Lavatory Handle
Acrylic
Chateau New Style

• For single handle faucet

Item #	Height (in)	Broach
ABRMO404-12S	1 ⅝	◻ (short)

MOEN*
Handle
Acrylic
Posi Temp

• For single handle faucet

Item #	Height (in)	Broach
ABRMO404-22L	1 ⅝	◻ (long)

NIBCO*
Cartridge
Plastic

NSF / ANSI 372 Compliant

Item #	Length (in)	Color	H/C	Broach
ABRNI11438	2.00	Black	C	3-7 (17pt)
ABRNI11439	2.00	White	H or C	3-7 (17pt)

NIBCO*
Cartridge
Plastic

Item #	Height (in)	Broach
ABRNI11440	4 1/16	⊤

NIBCO*
Tub & Shower Handle
Acrylic

Item #	Height (in)	Broach
ABRNI404-04	1 ⅝	⊤

NIBCO*
Handle Pair
Acrylic

• Also fits American Brass, Phoenix & Streamway

Item #	Height (in)	Broach
ABRNI408-14	1 1/16	3-7 (17pt)

NIBCO*
Face Plate
Chrome

Item #
ABRNI50336

NIBCO*
Teardrop Escutcheon Plate
Chrome

Item #	Length (in)	Width (in)
ABRNI50343	4 13/16	3 ⅛

NIBCO*
Escutcheon Extension
Plastic

Item #	Length (in)	Thread	Thread
ABRNI50338	2 11/16	1 11/16-18	15/16-18

NIBCO*
Stem Extension
Plastic

Item #	Length (in)	Internal Broach	External Broach
ABRNI50339	2 11/16	3-7 (17pt)	3-7 (17pt)

PHOENIX*
Stem
Brass

NSF / ANSI 372 Compliant

Item #	Length (in)	Broach	H/C
ABRPH11670-LF	1 9/16	3-7 (17pt)	H or C

PHOENIX*
Tub & Shower Handle
Acrylic
Lucite

• Also fits American Brass, Nibco & Streamway

Item #	Height (in)	Broach
ABRPH32760	1 ¾	3-7 (17pt)

To Order Call: 1.800.767.5552 . Fax: 1.800.886.9831

Original Mfg's names are used for identification only and are not a representation that the items offered are genuine items of the original Mfg.

BRASS
AMERICA
Quality Replacement Parts

PHOENIX*
Escutcheon
Chrome

Item #	O.D. (in)	Height (in)	Thread
ABRPH50328	2 ¾	1	1"-20

PHOENIX*
Flange
Chrome

Item #	O.D. (in)	Height (in)	Thread
ABRPH50333	1 ⅞	2 ¾	1"-20

PHOENIX*
Flange
Chrome

Item #	O.D. (in)	Height (in)	Thread
ABRPH50334	1 ³⁄₁₆	2 ⅜	¹⁵⁄₁₆-18

NSF / ANSI 372 Compliant

PRICE PFISTER*
Stem
Brass

• Includes gasket

Item #	Length (in)	Broach	H/C
ABRPP11635-LF	1 ⅝	1-2 (12pt)	H or C

NSF / ANSI 372 Compliant

PRICE PFISTER*
Stem
Brass

• Nickel plated stem
• Includes gasket

Item #	Length (in)	Broach	H/C
ABRPP11636-LF	1 ¹⁵⁄₁₆	1-2 (12pt)	Hot
ABRPP11637-LF	1 ¹⁵⁄₁₆	1-2 (12pt)	Cold

PRICE PFISTER*
Stem
Brass

• Includes gasket

Item #	Length (in)	Broach	H/C
ABRPP11640	2 ¹⁹⁄₃₂	1-12 (12pt)	H or C

PRICE PFISTER*
Diverter Stem
Brass

• Includes gasket

Item #	Length (in)	Broach
ABRPP11641	3 ⁵⁄₃₂	1-12 (12pt)

PRICE PFISTER*
Stem
Brass

NSF / ANSI 372 Compliant

• Chrome plated stem, includes gasket

Item #	Length (in)	Broach	H/C
ABRPP11665-LF	3 ¼	1-2 (12pt)	Hot
ABRPP11666-LF	3 ¼	1-2 (12pt)	Cold

PRICE PFISTER*
Stem
Ceramic

NSF / ANSI 372 Compliant

• Chrome plated unit, includes gasket

Item #	Length (in)	Broach	H/C
ABRPP11676-LF	1 ¾	1-2 (12pt)	H or C

PRICE PFISTER*
Single Lever Cartridge
Plastic
Avante

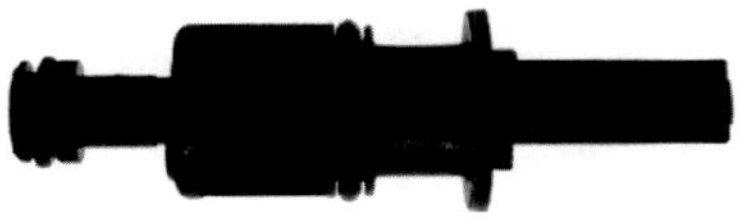

Item #	Length (in)	Broach	H/C
ABRPP11691	4 ⅛	⬡	H or C

PRICE PFISTER*
Stem
Brass

• Includes gasket

Item #	Length (in)	Broach	H/C
ABRPP21651	5 ½	1-2 (12pt)	H or C

PRICE PFISTER*
Diverter Stem
Brass

• Includes gasket

Item #	Length (in)	Broach
ABRPP21652	5.50	1-12 (12pt)

PRICE PFISTER*
Stem
Brass

• Includes gasket

Item #	Size (in)	Broach	H/C
ABRPP21653	5 ½	1-2 (12pt)	H or C

PRICE PFISTER*
Diverter Stem
Brass

• Includes gasket

Item #	Length (in)	Broach
ABRPP21654	5 ½	1-12 (12pt)

PRICE PFISTER*
Stem
Brass

• Includes gasket

Item #	Length (in)	Broach
ABRPP21655	4 ¼	1-12 (12pt)

To Order Call: 1.800.767.5552 . Fax: 1.800.886.9831

*Original Mfg's names are used for identification only and are not a representation that the items offered are genuine items of the original Mfg.

21

Quality Replacement Parts

PRICE PFISTER*
Diverter Stem
Brass

- *Includes gasket*

Item #	Length (in)	Broach
ABRPP21656	4 1/4	1-12 (12pt)

PRICE PFISTER*
Stem
Ceramic

- *Includes gasket*

Item #	Length (in)	Broach	H/C
ABRPP21670	4 1/8	1-2 (12pt)	H or C

PRICE PFISTER*
Tub & Shower Handle Pair
Chrome
Verve

Item #	Height (in)	Broach
ABRPP32800	2 1/2	1-2 (12pt)

PRICE PFISTER*
Diverter Handle
Chrome
Verve

Item #	Height (in)	Broach
ABRPP32800D	2 1/2	1-2 (12pt)

PRICE PFISTER*
Lav/Kit Handle Pair
Chrome
Verve
New Style

Item #	Height (in)	Broach
ABRPP32803	1 5/8	1-2 (12pt)

PRICE PFISTER*
Kitchen Handle Pair
Chrome
Dome

Item #	Height (in)	Broach
ABRPP32811	1 3/16	1-2 (12pt)

PRICE PFISTER*
Tub & Shower Handle Pair
Chrome
Contempra

Item #	Height (in)	Broach
ABRPP32840	2 1/2	1-2 (12pt)

PRICE PFISTER*
Diverter Handle
Chrome
Contempra

Item #	Height (in)	Broach
ABRPP32840D	2 1/2	1-2 (12pt)

PRICE PFISTER*
Lav/Kit Handle Pair
Chrome
Contempra

Item #	Height (in)	Broach
ABRPP32841	1 1/2	1-2 (12pt)

PRICE PFISTER*
Diverter Handle
Chrome
Crown Imperial

Item #	Height (in)	Broach
ABRPP32850D	3/4	1-2 (12pt)

PRICE PFISTER*
Lav/Kit Handle Pair
Chrome
Crown Imperial

Item #	Height (in)	Broach
ABRPP32860	7/8	1-2 (12pt)

PRICE PFISTER*
Cross Handle Pair
Chrome

Item #	Height (in)	Broach
ABRPP32870	13/16	1-2 (12pt)

PRICE PFISTER*
Diverter Handle
Chrome

Item #	Height (in)	Broach
ABRPP32870D	13/16	1-2 (12pt)

PRICE PFISTER*
Tub & Shower Handle Pair
Chrome
Crown Imperial

Item #	Height (in)	Broach
ABRPP32880	13/16	1-2 (12pt)

PRICE PFISTER*
Lav/Kit Handle Pair
Chrome
Verve

Item #	Height (in)	Broach
ABRPP32881	1 5/8	1-2 (12pt)

To Order Call: 1.800.767.5552 . Fax: 1.800.886.9831

Original Mfg's names are used for identification only and are not a representation that the items offered are genuine items of the original Mfg.

Quality Replacement Parts

PRICE PFISTER*
Lavatory Handle Pair
Chrome
Domel

Item #	Height (in)	Broach
ABRPP32882	15/16	1-2 (12pt)

PRICE PFISTER*
Tub & Shower Handle Pair
Chrome
Verve
New Style

Item #	Height (in)	Broach
ABRPP32883	2 1/2	1-2 (12pt)

PRICE PFISTER*
Diverter Handle
Chrome
Verve
New Style

Item #	Height (in)	Broach
ABRPP32883D	2 1/2	1-2 (12pt)

PRICE PFISTER*
Face Plate
Chrome

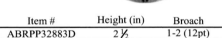

Item #
ABRPP35132

PRICE PFISTER*
Handle
Chrome
Flowmatic

Item #	Height (in)	Broach
ABRPP37156	3 3/4	

PRICE PFISTER*
Tub & Shower Handle
Acrylic
Avante

Item #	Height (in)	Broach
ABRPP404-09	2	

PRICE PFISTER*
Tub & Shower Handle
Acrylic
Avante Series 08 & 09

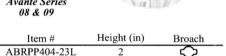

Item #	Height (in)	Broach
ABRPP404-23L	2	

PRICE PFISTER*
Tub & Shower Handle Pair
Acrylic
Windsor
• Chrome plated index included

Item #	Height (in)	Broach
ABRPP408-17	2 7/8	1-2 (12pt)

PRICE PFISTER*
Diverter Handle
Acrylic
Windsor
• Chrome plated index included

Item #	Height (in)	Broach
ABRPP408-17D	2 7/8	1-2 (12pt)

PRICE PFISTER*
Lav/Kit Handle Pair
Acrylic
Windsor
• Chrome plated index included

Item #	Height (in)	Broach
ABRPP408-19	1 3/4	1-2 (12pt)

PRICE PFISTER*
Tub & Shower Handle Pair
Acrylic
Marquis

Item #	Height (in)	Broach
ABRPP408-20	2 7/8	1-2 (12pt)

PRICE PFISTER*
Escutcheon
Chrome

Item #	O.D. (in)	Height (in)	Thread
ABRPP50342	2 1/2	1 11/16	21/32-18

PRICE PFISTER*
Escutcheon
Chrome

Item #	O.D. (in)	Height (in)	Thread
ABRPP50401	2 3/4	2 1/4	21/32-18

PRICE PFISTER*
Escutcheon
Chrome

Item #	O.D. (in)	Height (in)	Thread
ABRPP50402	2 1/2	1 1/4	1"-20

After all is said and done....
there's usually more said than done. ORDER NOW!

To Order Call: 1.800.767.5552 . Fax: 1.800.886.9831

*Original Mfg's names are used for identification only and are not a representation that the items offered are genuine items of the original Mfg.

23

Quality Replacement Parts

PRICE PFISTER*
Escutcheon
Chrome
- See ABRPP50412 for mating part

Item #	Length (in)	Width (in)	Height (in)
ABRPP50411	3 ⅞	2 ¾	2 ⅛

PRICE PFISTER*
Sleeve
Plastic
- See ABRPP50411 for mating part

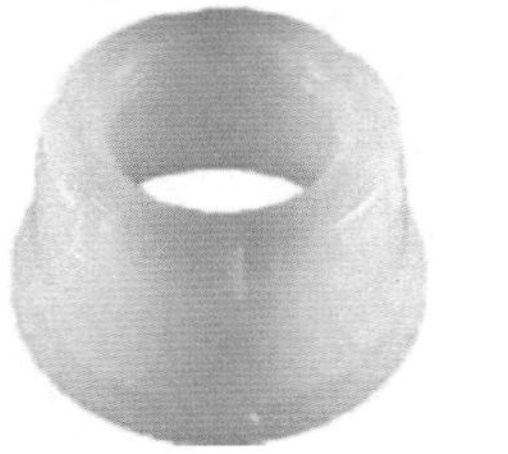

Item #	O.D. (in)	Height (in)	Thread
ABRPP50412	1 ³⁄₁₆	¾	²¹⁄₃₂-18

PRICE PFISTER*
Sleeve
Chrome
- See Fit-All ABRFA50326 for mating part

Item #	O.D. (in)	Length (in)	Thread
ABRPP50413	1 ¼	3 ¼	1 ¹³⁄₆₄-18

PRICE PFISTER*
Sleeve
Chrome
- See Fit-All ABRFA50326 for mating part

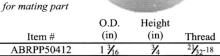

Item #	O.D. (in)	Length (in)	Thread
ABRPP50414	1 ¼	2	1 ¹³⁄₆₄-18

PRICE PFISTER*
Index Button
1 9/16" O.D.
04-09 Avante

Item #
ABRPP704-09-1

PRICE PFISTER*
Index Button
15/16" O.D.

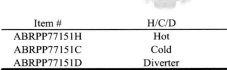

Item #	H/C/D
ABRPP77151H	Hot
ABRPP77151C	Cold
ABRPP77151D	Diverter

PRICE PFISTER*
Index Button
Chrome
Verve

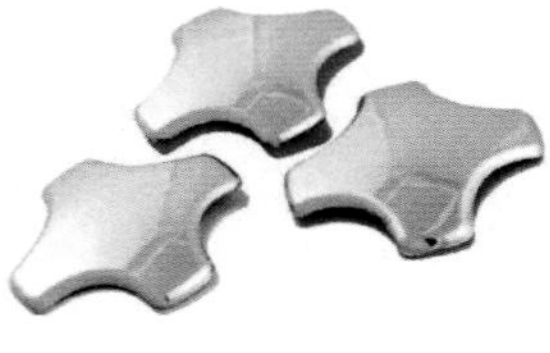

Item #	H/C/D
ABRPP77152H	Hot
ABRPP77152C	Cold
ABRPP77152D	Diverter

PRICE PFISTER*
Index Button
1 1/8" O.D.

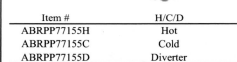

Item #	H/C/D
ABRPP77155H	Hot
ABRPP77155C	Cold
ABRPP77155D	Diverter

PRICE PFISTER*
Nipple
Plastic

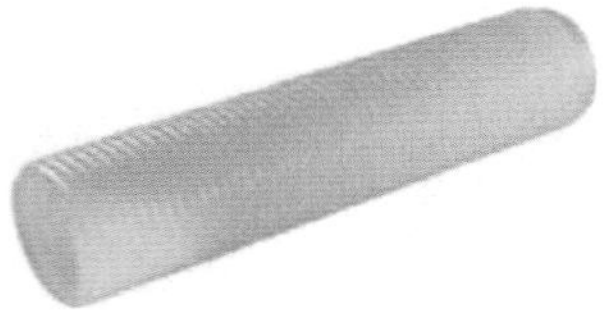

Item #	Length (in)	TPI
ABRPP213218L	2 ¾	²¹⁄₃₂-18

PRICE PFISTER*
Hydro-Seal Seat Washer 
- Fits all Price Pfister Hydro-Seal units

Item #
ABRPP-SEAT

SAVOY*
Stem
Brass

- Chrome plated stem, includes gasket

Item #	Length (in)	Broach	H/C
ABRSV21961	5 ⅛	1-13 (15pt)	H or C

SAVOY*
Stem
Brass

- Includes gasket

Item #	Length (in)	Broach	H/C
ABRSV21962	4 ¹⁹⁄₃₂	1-13 (15pt)	H or C

SAVOY*
Stem
Brass

- Chrome plated stem & sleeve

Item #	Length (in)	Broach	H/C
ABRSV21964	5 ¾	1-13 (15pt)	H or C

SAVOY*
Stem
Brass

- Chrome plated stem, sleeve
- Includes gasket

Item #	Length (in)	Broach	H/C
ABRSV21968	5 ¹³⁄₁₆	1-13 (15pt)	H or C

SAVOY*
Stem
Brass

- Includes gasket

Item #	Length (in)	Broach	H/C
ABRSV21970	3 ¹³⁄₁₆	1-13 (15pt)	H or C

To Order Call: 1.800.767.5552 . Fax: 1.800.886.9831

Original Mfg's names are used for identification only and are not a representation that the items offered are genuine items of the original Mfg.

SAVOY*
Diverter Stem
Brass

• Includes gasket

Item #	Length (in)	Broach
ABRSV21972	5 15/16	1-13 (15pt)

SAVOY*
Handle Pair
Chrome

Item #	Height (in)	Broach
ABRSV32911	1 5/8	1-13 (15pt)

SAVOY*
Diverter Handle
Chrome

Item #	Height (in)	Broach
ABRSV32911D	1 5/8	1-13 (15pt)

SAVOY*
Cross Handle
Chrome

Item #	Height (in)	Broach
ABRSV33248	9/16	1-13 (15pt)

SAVOY*
Sleeve
Threaded

• See Fit-All
ABRFA50330 for mating part

Item #	O.D. (in)	Length (in)	Thread
ABRSV50368	1 1/16	2 3/4	1"-20

SAVOY*
Escutcheon
Chrome

Item #	O.D. (in)	Height (in)	Thread
ABRSV52912	1 7/8	7/8	1 1/16-18

NSF / ANSI 372
Compliant

SAYCO*
Stem
Brass

• Nickel plated gland

Item #	Length (in)	Broach	H/C
ABRSA11938-LF	1 17/32	2-3 (16pt)	Hot
ABRSA11939-LF	1 17/32	2-3 (16pt)	Cold

SAYCO*
Stem
Brass

Item #	Length (in)	Broach	H/C
ABRSA21951	4 1/2	2-3 (16pt)	Hot
ABRSA21952	4 1/2	2-3 (16pt)	Cold

SAYCO*
Diverter Stem
Brass

Item #	Length (in)	Broach
ABRSA21953	4 1/2	2-3 (16pt)

SAYCO*
Stem
Brass

• Includes gasket

Item #	Length (in)	Broach	H/C
ABRSA21957	4 15/16	2-3 (16pt)	H or C

SAYCO*
Tub & Shower Handle Pair
Chrome

Item #	Height (in)	Broach
ABRSA33030	2 1/4	2-3 (16pt)

SAYCO*
Diverter Handle
Chrome

Item #	Height (in)	Broach
ABRSA33030D	2 1/4	2-3 (16pt)

SAYCO*
Tub & Shower Handle Pair
Chrome

Item #	Height (in)	Broach
ABRSA33031	1 1/2	2-3 (16pt)

SAYCO*
Diverter Handle
Chrome

Item #	Height (in)	Broach
ABRSA33031D	1 1/2	2-3 (16pt)

MORE INSPIRATION
Only those who do nothing at all make no mistakes, but that would be a mistake...SO SEND AN ORDER!

To Order Call: 1.800.767.5552 . Fax: 1.800.886.9831

Original Mfg's names are used for identification only and are not a representation that the items offered are genuine items of the original Mfg.

25

Quality Replacement Parts

SAYCO*
Lav/Kit Handle Pair
Chrome

Item #	Height (in)	Broach
ABRSA33033	1 5/8	2-3 (16pt)

SAYCO*
Escutcheon
Chrome

Item #	Length (in)	I.D. (in)	Width (in)
ABRSA50371	4 5/16	1 1/4	2 13/16

SAYCO*
Sleeve
Chrome

Item #	O.D. (in)	Length (in)	Thread
ABRSA50372	1 7/8	3	1 1/16-20

SAYCO*
Escutcheon
Chrome

Item #	O.D. (in)	I.D. (in)	Height (in)
ABRSA50391	2 3/4	1 1/4	5/8

Send Your ABRASS Orders To:

BARRY E. WALTER SR. CO.

Fax or E-mail:
orderdesk@barrywalter.com

SAYCO*
Index Button
1 1/4" O.D.

Item #	H/C/D
ABRSA77162H	Hot
ABRSA77162C	Cold
ABRSA77162D	Diverter

SPEAKMAN*
Stem
Ceramic

Item #	Length (in)	Broach	H/C
ABRSP29200H	3 37/64	3-14 (20pt)	Hot
ABRSP29200C	3 37/64	3-14 (20pt)	Cold

SPEAKMAN*
Tub & Shower Handle Pair
Chrome

Item #	Height (in)	Broach
ABRSP33111	1 3/4	2-4 (20pt)

SPEAKMAN*
Diverter Handle
Chrome

Item #	Height (in)	Broach
ABRSP33111D	1 3/4	2-4 (20pt)

STERLING*
Stem
Brass

• *Includes gasket*

Item #	Length (in)	Broach	H/C
ABRSL11965	2 3/8	1-5 (16pt)	Hot

STERLING*
Stem
Brass

• *Includes gasket*

Item #	Size (in)	Broach	H/C
ABRSL21981	4 11/16	1-5 (16pt)	H or C

STERLING*
Diverter Stem
Brass

• *Includes gasket*

Item #	Length (in)	Broach
ABRSL21982	4 5/8	1-5 (16pt)

STERLING*
Stem
Brass

• *Chrome plated stem, includes gasket*

Item #	Length (in)	Broach	H/C
ABRSL21983	5 3/8	1-5 (16pt)	H or C

STERLING*
Stem
Brass

Item #	Length (in)	Broach	H/C
ABRSL21986	4 3/8	1-5 (16pt)	H or C

STERLING*
Diverter Stem
Brass

Item #	Length (in)	Broach
ABRSL21987	5 1/16	1-5 (16pt)

To Order Call: 1.800.767.5552 . Fax: 1.800.886.9831

*Original Mfg's names are used for identification only and are not a representation that the items offered are genuine items of the original Mfg.

STERLING*
Stem
Brass

• *Includes o-ring*

Item #	Length (in)	Broach	H/C
ABRSL21994	4 ½	Square	H or C

STERLING*
Stem
Brass

• *Includes o-ring*

Item #	Length (in)	Broach	H/C
ABRSL21995	3 ²³⁄₃₂	Square	H or C

STERLING*
Handle Pair
Chrome

Item #	Height (in)	Broach
ABRSL32886	½	1-5 (16pt)

STERLING*
Kit/Lav
Handle Pair
Chrome

Item #	Height (in)	Broach
ABRSL32890	⅞	1-5 (16pt)

STERLING*
Diverter
Handle
Chrome

Item #	Height (in)	Broach
ABRSL32890D	⅞	1-5 (16pt)

STERLING*
Handle Pair
Chrome

Item #	Height (in)	Broach
ABRSL33210	1 ½	1-5 (16pt)

STERLING*
Diverter
Handle
Chrome

Item #	Height (in)	Broach
ABRSL33210D	1 ½	1-5 (16pt)

STERLING*
Handle Pair
Chrome

Item #	Height (in)	Broach
ABRSL33240	1 ¼	1-5 (16pt)

STERLING*
Kit/Lav
Handle Pair
Chrome

Item #	Height (in)	Broach
ABRSL33241	1 ¼	1-5 (16pt)

STERLING*
Diverter
Handle
Chrome

Item #	Height (in)	Broach
ABRSL33241D	1 ¼	1-5 (16pt)

STERLING*
Handle Pair
Chrome

Item #	Height (in)	Broach
ABRSL33242	1 ½	1-5 (16pt)

STERLING*
Diverter
Handle
Chrome

Item #	Height (in)	Broach
ABRSL33242D	1 ½	1-5 (16pt)

STERLING*
Handle Pair
Chrome

Item #	Height (in)	Broach
ABRSL33243	2 ¼	1-5 (16pt)

STERLING*
Diverter
Handle
Chrome

Item #	Height (in)	Broach
ABRSL33243D	2 ¼	1-5 (16pt)

STERLING*
Handle Pair
Chrome

Item #	Height (in)	Broach
ABRSL33245	⁹⁄₁₆	1-5 (16pt)

To Order Call: 1.800.767.5552 . Fax: 1.800.886.9831

*Original Mfg's names are used for identification only and are not a representation that the items offered are genuine items of the original Mfg.   27

Quality Replacement Parts

STERLING*
Handle Pair
Acrylic

Item #	Height (in)	Broach
ABRSL408-11	2 1/8	Square

STERLING*
Diverter Handle
Acrylic

Item #	Height (in)	Broach
ABRSL408-11D	2 1/8	Square

STERLING*
Lavatory Handle Pair
Acrylic

Item #	Height (in)	Broach
ABRSL408-12	2 1/8	1-5 (16pt)

STERLING*
Tub & Shower Handle Pair
Acrylic

Item #	Height (in)	Broach
ABRSL408-44	2 5/8	1-5 (16pt)

STERLING*
Diverter Handle
Acrylic

Item #	Height (in)	Broach
ABRSL408-44D	2 5/8	1-5 (16pt)

STERLING*
Nipple
Plastic

Item #	Lenght (in)	TPI
ABRSL50366L	2 11/16	3/4-16

STERLING*
Escutcheon
Chrome

Item #	O.D. (in)	Height (in)	Thread
ABRSL50375	2 1/4	15/32	1 1/8-18

STERLING*
Escutcheon
Chrome

Item #	O.D. (in)	Height (in)	Thread
ABRSL50376	2 1/4	9/16	1 1/16-20

STERLING*
Escutcheon
Chrome

Item #	O.D. (in)	Height (in)	Thread
ABRSL50388	2 1/2	1	15/16-20

STERLING*
Sleeve
Chrome

• *See ABRFA50326 for mating part*

Item #	O.D. (in)	Length (in)	Thread
ABRSL50423	1 1/4	2 1/8	1 7/32-28

STERLING*
Sleeve
Chrome

• *See ABRFA50326 for mating part*

Item #	O.D. (in)	Length (in)	Thread
ABRSL50424	1 1/4	2 1/2	1 7/32-28

STERLING*
Index Button
1 1/8" O.D.

Item #	H/C/D
ABRSL77171H	Hot
ABRSL77171C	Cold
ABRSL77171D	Diverter

STERLING*
Index Button
1 1/8" O.D.

Item #	H/C/D
ABRSL77172H	Hot
ABRSL77172C	Cold
ABRSL77172D	Diverter

STERLING*
Index Button
1 9/16" O.D.

Item #
ABRSL77173

STREAMWAY*
Stem
Brass

✓ *NSF / ANSI 372 Compliant*

• *Includes gasket*

Item #	Length (in)	Broach	H/C
ABRSW11911-LF	1 5/8	3-7 (17pt)	Hot
ABRSW11912-LF	1 5/8	3-7 (17pt)	Cold

To Order Call: 1.800.767.5552 . Fax: 1.800.886.9831

Original Mfg's names are used for identification only and are not a representation that the items offered are genuine items of the original Mfg.

Quality Replacement Parts

STREAMWAY*
Handle Pair
Chrome

- Also fits American Brass, Nibco & Phoenix

Item #	Height (in)	Broach
ABRSW32900	1 7/8	3-7 (17pt)

STREAMWAY*
Handle Pair
Chrome

- Also fits American Brass, Nibco & Phoenix

Item #	Height (in)	Broach
ABRSW33330	1 1/4	3-7 (17pt)

SYMMONS*
Tub & Shower Handle
Chrome
Temptrol

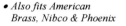

- See ABRSY77210 for index button
- OEM#: T-31

Item #	Height (in)
ABRSY37210	1 1/4

SYMMONS*
Tub & Shower Handle
Chrome
Safety Mix

- OEM#: RC-14

Item #	Height (in)	Skirt
ABRSY37220	1 1/2	Long

SYMMONS*
Tub & Shower Handle
Chrome
Temptrol

- OEM#: RC-14X

Item #	Height (in)	Length (in)	Skirt
ABRSY37221	7/8	4 1/4	Short

SYMMONS*
Diverter Handle
Chrome
Temptrol

- OEM#: T-30

Item #	Height (in)
ABRSY37230	2

SYMMONS*
Kitchen Handle
Chrome

- Single lever
- OEM#: K-3

Item #	Height (in)	Length (in)
ABRSY37231	1	4

SYMMONS*
Lav Handle
Chrome

- Single lever
- OEM#: L-2

Item #	Length (in)
ABRSY37232	3

SYMMONS*
Index Button
Chrome

- For ABRSY37210

Item #
ABRSY77210

T & S*
Barrel
Brass

✓ NSF / ANSI 372 Compliant

- Also fits Binford

Item #	Lenght (in)	H/C
ABRTS12001-LF	1 17/32	Hot
ABRTS12002-LF	1 17/32	Cold

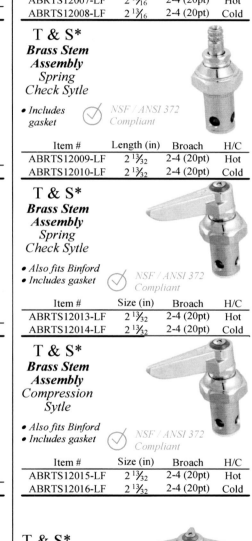

T & S*
Brass Stem Assembly
Compression Sytle

✓ NSF / ANSI 372 Compliant

- Also fits Binford

Item #	Size (in)	Broach	H/C
ABRTS12007-LF	2 13/16	2-4 (20pt)	Hot
ABRTS12008-LF	2 13/16	2-4 (20pt)	Cold

T & S*
Brass Stem Assembly
Spring Check Sytle

- Includes gasket

✓ NSF / ANSI 372 Compliant

Item #	Length (in)	Broach	H/C
ABRTS12009-LF	2 13/32	2-4 (20pt)	Hot
ABRTS12010-LF	2 13/32	2-4 (20pt)	Cold

T & S*
Brass Stem Assembly
Spring Check Sytle

- Also fits Binford
- Includes gasket

✓ NSF / ANSI 372 Compliant

Item #	Size (in)	Broach	H/C
ABRTS12013-LF	2 13/32	2-4 (20pt)	Hot
ABRTS12014-LF	2 13/32	2-4 (20pt)	Cold

T & S*
Brass Stem Assembly
Compression Sytle

- Also fits Binford
- Includes gasket

✓ NSF / ANSI 372 Compliant

Item #	Size (in)	Broach	H/C
ABRTS12015-LF	2 13/32	2-4 (20pt)	Hot
ABRTS12016-LF	2 13/32	2-4 (20pt)	Cold

T & S*
Handle Pair
Chrome

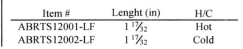

- Also fits Speakman

Item #	Width (in)	Broach
ABRTS32953	2 3/8	2-4 (20pt)

Quality Replacement Parts

T & S*
Diverter Handle
Chrome

• *Also fits Speakman*

Item #	Width (in)	Broach
ABRTS32953D	2 ⅜	2-4 (20pt)

T & S*
ADA Handle Pair
Chrome
• *Also fits Speakman*

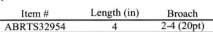

Item #	Length (in)	Broach
ABRTS32954	4	2-4 (20pt)

T & S*
Handle
Chrome

• *Also fits Binford & Speakman*

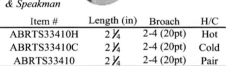

Item #	Length (in)	Broach	H/C
ABRTS33410H	2 ¼	2-4 (20pt)	Hot
ABRTS33410C	2 ¼	2-4 (20pt)	Cold
ABRTS33410	2 ¼	2-4 (20pt)	Pair

T & S*
Index Button
5/8" O.D.

Item #	H/C	Color
ABRTS77178H	Hot	Red
ABRTS77178C	Cold	Blue

T & S*
Index Ring
9/16" O.D.

• *Also fits Binford*

Item #	H/C	Color
ABRTS77190H	Hot	Red
ABRTS77190C	Cold	Blue

NSF / ANSI 372 Compliant

T & S*
Hose
Pre-Rinse

• *Also fits Binford pre-rinse units*
• *Includes T&S, Fisher & Chicago adapters*

Item #	Length (in)
ABR3612-HOSE-LF	44

NSF / ANSI 372 Compliant

T & S*
Spray Head
Pre-Rinse

• *Also fits Binford pre-rinse units*

Item #
ABR3612-SPRAY-LF

T & S*
Spring
Pre-Rinse

• *Also fits Binford, T&S, Chicago, CHG & Fisher*

Item #	Length (mm)
ABR3612-SPRING	670

NSF / ANSI 372 Compliant

T & S*
Vacuum Breaker Kit

• *For SVC Faucets*
• *Fits ABF3050 & ABF3055*

Item #
ABRTSKIT-VB-LF

UNION BRASS*
Stem
Brass

NSF / ANSI 372 Compliant

• *Includes gasket*

Item #	Length (in)	Broach	H/C
ABRUN12101-LF	1 ⁹⁄₁₆	3-3 (18pt)	Hot
ABRUN12102-LF	1 ⁹⁄₁₆	3-3 (18pt)	Cold

UNION BRASS*
Stem
Ceramic

NSF / ANSI 372 Compliant

• *Includes gasket*

Item #	Length (in)	Broach	H/C
ABRUN12156-LF	1 ⁷⁄₁₆	3-3 (18pt)	Hot
ABRUN12157-LF	1 ⁷⁄₁₆	3-3 (18pt)	Cold

UNION BRASS*
Stem
Ceramic

• *Flip plastic stop for ADA cold stem*
• *Includes gasket*

Item #	Length (in)	Broach	H/C
ABRUN22109	3 ⁵⁄₁₆	3-3 (18pt)	H or C

UNION BRASS*
Stem
Brass

• *Includes gasket*

Item #	Size (in)	Broach	H/C
ABRUN22110	3 ¼	3-3 (18pt)	Hot
ABRUN22111	3 ¼	3-3 (18pt)	Cold

UNION BRASS*
Stem
Brass

• *Includes gasket*

Item #	Size (in)	Broach	H/C
ABRUN22112	3 ⁵⁄₁₆	3-3 (18pt)	Hot
ABRUN22113	3 ⁵⁄₁₆	3-3 (18pt)	Cold

UNION BRASS*
Diverter Stem
Brass

Item #	Length (in)	Broach
ABRUN22117	4 ⅝	D

To Order Call: 1.800.767.5552 . Fax: 1.800.886.9831

*Original Mfg's names are used for identification only and are not a representation that the items offered are genuine items of the original Mfg.

Quality Replacement Parts

BRASS
AMERICA
Quality Replacement Parts

UNION BRASS*
Diverter Stem
Brass

Item #	Length (in)	Broach
ABRUN22119	4 ¾	D

UNION BRASS*
Handle Pair
Chrome

• *Also fits Briggs & Indiana*

Item #	Height (in)	Broach
ABRUN33510	1 ⁵⁄₁₆	3-3 (18pt)

UNION BRASS*
Diverter Handle
Chrome

• *Also fits Briggs & Indiana*

Item #	Height (in)	Broach
ABRUN33510D	1 ⁵⁄₁₆	3-3 (18pt)

UNION BRASS*
Diverter Handle
Chrome

Item #	Height (in)	Broach
ABRUN33510DA	1 ⁵⁄₁₆	"D"

UNION BRASS*
Kitchen Handle Pair
Chrome

• *Also fits Briggs & Indiana*

Item #	Height (in)	Broach
ABRUN33511	1 ¼	3-3 (18pt)

UNION BRASS*
Lavatory Handle Pair
Chrome

• *Also fits Briggs & Indiana*

Item #	Height (in)	Broach
ABRUN33512	1	3-3 (18pt)

UNION BRASS*
Diverter Handle
Chrome

• *Also fits Briggs & Indiana*

Item #	Height (in)	Broach
ABRUN33513D	1 ⅜	3-3 (18pt)

UNION BRASS*
Lav/Kit Handle Pair
Chrome

• *Also fits Briggs & Indiana*

Item #	Height (in)	Broach
ABRUN33530	1	3-3 (18pt)

UNION BRASS*
Handle Pair
Chrome

• *Also fits Briggs & Indiana*

Item #	Height (in)	Broach
ABRUN33531	1 ¹⁵⁄₁₆	3-3 (18pt)

UNION BRASS*
Tub & Shower Handle Pair
Chrome

• *Also fits Briggs & Indiana*

Item #	Height (in)	Broach
ABRUN33532	1 ¼	3-3 (18pt)

UNION BRASS*
Escutcheon
Chrome

• *For mating part see ABRUN50442*

Item #	O.D. (in)	I.D. (in)	Height (in)
ABRUN50441	1 ⅜	¾	1 ⅜

UNION BRASS*
Sleeve
Chrome

• *For mating part see ABRUN50441*

Item #	Length (in)	Thread
ABRUN50442	1 ⅛	⅝-24

UNION BRASS*
Nipple
Brass

Item #	Length (in)	TPI
ABRUN50443	1 ⅜	⅝-24

VALLEY*
Cartridge
Plastic

 NSF / ANSI 372 Compliant

Item #	Length (in)	Broach	H/C
ABRVA12241	2 ¹⁷⁄₃₂	D	H or C

VALLEY*
Single Lever Cartridge
Plastic
404-20

• *Use with spray*

Item #	Size (in)	Broach
ABRVA12246	2 ⅜	O

To Order Call: 1.800.767.5552 . Fax: 1.800.886.9831

*Original Mfg's names are used for identification only and are not a representation that the items offered are genuine items of the original Mfg.

31

VALLEY*
Single Lever Cartridge
Plastic

• *Use without spray*

Item #	Length (in)	Broach
ABRVA12247	2 ⅜	O

VALLEY*
Cartridge
Plastic

Item #	Length (in)	Broach	H/C
ABRVA12248	2 ⁵⁄₁₆	O	H or C

VALLEY*
Cartridge
Plastic

NSF / ANSI 372
Compliant

Item #	Length (in)	Broach	H/C
ABRVA12249	1 ²⁷⁄₃₂	D	H or C

VALLEY*
Handle
Chrome

Item #	Broach	Type
ABRVA33810	O	Old Style

VALLEY*
Handle
Chrome

Item #	Broach	Type
ABRVA33811	O	New Style

VALLEY*
Tub & Shower Handle
Acrylic

Item #	Height (in)	Broach	Type
ABRVA404-15	1 ⅜	O	Old Style

VALLEY*
Tub & Shower Handle
Acrylic

• *Ring and set screwincluded*

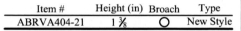

Item #	Height (in)	Broach	Type
ABRVA404-21	1 ⅜	O	New Style

VALLEY*
Tub & Shower Handle Pair
Acrylic

Item #	Height (in)	Broach
ABRVA408-01	3	D

VALLEY*
Lav/Kit Handle Pair
Acrylic

Item #	Height (in)	Broach
ABRVA408-02	1 ¾	D

VALLEY*
Index Button
1" O.D.

• *Fits ABRVA404-21*

Item #
ABRVA704-20-1

VALLEY*
Index Button
1" O.D.

Item #	H/C
ABRVA7408-01BNC	Cold
ABRVA7408-01BNH	Hot

VALLEY*
Seat Kit

• *Inserts and springs included*

Item #
ABRVA-KIT1

WOODFORD*
Wall Hydrant Handle
Metal

• *For models 14 & 17*

Item #
ABRWF32061

Send Your ABRASS Orders To:

BARRY E. WALTER SR. CO.

Fax or E-mail:
orderdesk@barrywalter.com

---

*Original Mfg's names are used for identification only and are not a representation that the items offered are genuine items of the original Mfg.

GLACIER BAY*
Cartridge
Ceramic

NSF / ANSI 372 Compliant

- *Also fits various manufacturers*

Item #	Length (in)	Broach	H/C
ABRCC19019-LF	1 7/8	3-18 (24pt)	Hot
ABRCC19020-LF	1 7/8	3-18 (24pt)	Cold

GLACIER BAY*
Cartridge
Ceramic

NSF / ANSI 372 Compliant

- *Also fits various manufacturers*

Item #	Length (in)	Broach	H/C
ABRIM13801-LF	1 7/8	"D"	Hot
ABRIM13802-LF	1 7/8	"D"	Cold

NSF / ANSI 372 Compliant

PRICE PFISTER*
Single Lever Cartridge
Ceramic
- *OEM: 974-074*
- *Also fits various manufacturers*

Item #	Dia.	Height
ABRCC19001	25mm	50mm

NSF / ANSI 372 Compliant

IMPORT
Hot or Cold Cartridge
Ceramic
- *OEM: GL02GJ-004*
- *Fits various manufacturers*

Item #	Dia.	Height
ABRCC19002	25mm	49mm

NSF / ANSI 372 Compliant

IMPORT
Diverter Cartridge
Ceramic
with brass spindle
- *Fits various manufacturers*

Item #	Dia.	Height
ABRCC19003	22mm	42mm

Single Lever Cartridge
Ceramic

Item #	Dia.	Height
Use ABRCC19006	35mm	56mm

NSF / ANSI 372 Compliant

SAYCO*
Single Lever Cartridge
Ceramic
- *Also fits Eljer, Ez-Flo and others*

Item #	Dia.	Height
ABRCC19006	35mm	57mm

Single Lever Cartridge
Ceramic

Item #	Dia.	Height
Use ABRCC19006	35mm	57mm

NSF / ANSI 372 Compliant

PRICE PFISTER*
Single Lever Cartridge
Ceramic
- *Also fits Delta, Kingston and others*

Item #	Dia.	Height
ABRCC19008	35mm	70mm

NSF / ANSI 372 Compliant

IMPORT
Single Lever Cartridge
Ceramic
- *Fits various manufacturers*

Item #	Dia.	Height
ABRCC19010	35mm	71mm

NSF / ANSI 372 Compliant

IMPORT
Single Lever Cartridge
Ceramic
- *Fits various manufacturers*

Item #	Dia.	Height
ABRCC19011	35mm	58mm

NSF / ANSI 372 Compliant

SYMMONS*
Single Lever Cartridge
Ceramic
- *Also fits Zurn RK7440, Ez-Flo, Union Brass & others*

Item #	Dia.	Height
ABRCC19012	40mm	63mm

JADO*
Single Lever Cartridge
Ceramic

Item #	Dia.	Height
Use ABRCC19012	40mm	63mm

NSF / ANSI 372 Compliant

PRICE PFISTER*
Single Lever Cartridge
Ceramic
- *Also fits Danze & others*

Item #	Dia.	Height
ABRCC19014	40mm	76mm

EZ-FLO*
Single Lever Pressure Balance Cartridge
Ceramic
- *Also fits ProFlo & others*

Item #	Dia.	Height
ABRCC19015	40mm	87mm

To Order Call: 1.800.767.5552 . Fax: 1.800.886.9831

*Original Mfg's names are used for identification only and are not a representation that the items offered are genuine items of the original Mfg. 33

IMPORT
Single Lever Cartridge
Ceramic

 NSF / ANSI 372 Compliant

- Fits various manufacturers

Item #	Dia.	Height
ABRCC19016	40mm	74mm

IMPORT
Single Lever Cartridge
Ceramic

 NSF / ANSI 372 Compliant

- Fits various manufacturers

Item #	Dia.	Height
ABRCC19017	40mm	61mm

HUNTINGTON*
Single Lever Pressure Balance Cartridge
Ceramic

- 13/32" square broach

Item #	Dia.	Height
ABRCC19023-OS	40mm	79mm

HUNTINGTON*
Single Lever Pressure Balance Cartridge
Ceramic

- 23/64" square broach

Item #	Dia.	Height
ABRCC19023SP	40mm	79mm

EZ-FLO*
Single Lever Pressure Balance Cartridge
Ceramic

Item #	Dia.	Height
ABRCC19024	40mm	78mm

IMPORT
Single Lever Pressure Balance Cartridge
Ceramic

Item #	Dia.	Height
ABRCC19025	40mm	75mm

ZURN*
Single Lever Pressure Balance Cartridge
Ceramic

- OEM: RK7300-CART-3P
- Also fits Glacier Bay & others

Item #	Dia.	Height
ABRCC19025-OS	40mm	75mm

HYDROPLAST
Single Lever Cartridge
Ceramic

- OEM: B35
- Also fits Jado, Jaclo & others

 NSF / ANSI 372 Compliant

Item #	Dia.	Height
ABRCC19026	36mm	58mm

CONCINNITY/ JACLO*
Single Lever Cartridge
Ceramic

 NSF / ANSI 372 Compliant

Item #	Dia.	Height
ABRCC19027	35mm	57mm

 NSF / ANSI 372 Compliant

PAIJO
Single Lever Cartridge
Ceramic

- Fits various manufacturers

Item #	Dia.	Height
ABRCC19028	25mm	61mm

SEASONS*
Single Lever Pressure Balance Cartridge
Ceramic

- Also fits Glacier Bay & others

Item #	Dia.	Height
ABRCC19029	40mm	130mm

HUNTINGTON
Single Lever Pressure Balance Cartridge

- OEM: ST5000C

Item #	Dia.	Height
ABRCC19030	47mm	89mm

HUNTINGTON
Single Lever Cartridge

NSF / ANSI 372 Compliant

- OEM: ST5000

Item #	Height
ABRCC19031	51mm

GLACIER BAY/ PEGASUS*
Single Lever Pressure Balance Cartridge
Ceramic

- OEM: 10321
- Also fits Premier & others

Item #	Dia.	Height
ABRCC19032	40mm	75mm

GLACIER BAY*
Single Lever Pressure Balance Cartridge
Ceramic

- Also fits Aqua Source

Item #	Dia.	Height
ABRCC19033	40mm	83mm

To Order Call: 1.800.767.5552 . Fax: 1.800.886.9831

*Original Mfg's names are used for identification only and are not a representation that the items offered are genuine items of the original Mfg.

Quality Replacement Parts

Quality Replacement Parts

HYDROPLAST
Single Lever Cartridge
Ceramic

NSF / ANSI 372 Compliant

- OEM: G35
- Also fits Kohler, Wolverine & others

Item #	Dia.	Height
ABRCC19034	35mm	57mm

HYDROPLAST
Single Lever Cartridge
Ceramic

NSF / ANSI 372 Compliant

- OEM: GX35
- Also fits Kohler & others

Item #	Dia.	Height
ABRCC19035	35mm	70mm

HYDROPLAST
Single Lever Cartridge
Ceramic

NSF / ANSI 372 Compliant

- OEM: G40
- Fits various manufacteres

Item #	Dia.	Height
ABRCC19036	40mm	64mm

NSF / ANSI 372 Compliant

PRICE PFISTER*
Single Lever Cartridge
Ceramic

- OEM: 974-505

Item #	Dia.	Height
ABRCC19037	35mm	63mm

NSF / ANSI 372 Compliant

PRICE PFISTER*
Single Lever Cartridge
Ceramic

- OEM: 974-0350

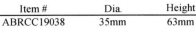

Item #	Dia.	Height
ABRCC19038	35mm	63mm

SAYCO
Single Lever Pressure Balance Cartridge
Ceramic

- OEM: P1070

Item #	Dia.	Height
ABRCC19039	38mm	78mm

SAYCO
Single Lever Pressure Balance Cartridge
Ceramic

- OEM: P1071
- Also fits Kingston & Webstone

Item #	Dia.	Height
ABRCC19040	38mm	76mm

SAYCO*
Single Lever Pressure Balance Cartridge
Ceramic

- OEM: R200CC

Item #	Dia.	Height
ABRCC19041	46mm	85mm

NSF / ANSI 372 Compliant

SAYCO
Single Lever Pressure Balance Cartridge
Ceramic

- OEM: P1050

Item #	Dia.	Height
ABRCC19042	38mm	62mm

SAYCO
Single Lever Pressure Balance Cartridge
Ceramic

- OEM: P1079

Item #	Dia.	Height
ABRCC19043	38mm	88mm

NSF / ANSI 372 Compliant

STARLIGHT*
Single Lever Pressure Balance Cartridge
Ceramic

- Also fits Moen & others

Item #	Dia.	Height
ABRCC19044	40mm	63mm

CFG*
Single Lever Pressure Balance Cartridge
Ceramic

- OEM: 40068

Item #	Dia.	Height
ABRCC19045	40mm	76mm

CFG*
Single Lever Pressure Balance Cartridge
Ceramic

- OEM: 40069

Item #	Dia.	Height
ABRCC19046	40mm	76mm

PRO FLO
Single Lever Pressure Balance Cartridge
Ceramic

- OEM: ACF3001CRT

Item #	Dia.	Height
ABRCC19047	40mm	85mm

WOLVERINE
Single Lever Pressure Balance Cartridge
Ceramic

Item #	Dia.	Height
ABRCC19048	40mm	84mm

To Order Call: 1.800.767.5552 . Fax: 1.800.886.9831

Original Mfg's names are used for identification only and are not a representation that the items offered are genuine items of the original Mfg.

NSF / ANSI 372 Compliant

WOLVERINE
Single Lever Cartridge
Ceramic

Item #	Dia.	Height
ABRCC19049	35mm	58mm

EZ-FLO*
Single Lever Pressure Balance Cartridge
Ceramic

• Also fits ProFlo, Gerber & others

Item #	Dia.	Height
ABRPBCV	40mm	85mm

NSF / ANSI 372 Compliant

GERBER*
Tub & Shower Cartridge

• OEM: 95-154
• Also fits B&K, Matco-Norca & others

Item #
ABRPBCV-CTG

GERBER*
Mixer
Single Lever

• OEM: 95-152
• For pressure balance control valve
• Also fits B&K, EZ-Flo & others

Item #
ABRPBCV-MIX

SAYCO*
Mixer
Single Lever

• Also fits Huntington

Item #
ABRCC-MIX

Temperature Setting Ring
Rubber

• Use with ABRP-BCV-CTG
• For pressure balance control valve

Item #
ABRPBCV-RING

Single Lever Handles

SAYCO*
Lav / T&S Handle
Chrome

• Fits most single lever cartridges with square broaches

Item #	Broach
ABRSA33038	☐

BINFORD*
Loop Handle
Chrome

• Fits Binford 5371L faucet
• Fits ABRPBCV-CTG

Item #
ABR5371L-HDL

BINFORD*
Lav / T&S Handle
Chrome

• Fits Binford 5310LS & 5510LS faucets
• Also fits most faucets that use the Delta #70 ball

Item #	Broach
ABR5510LS-HDL	◯

MIXET*
Loop Handle
Chrome

• Fits ABRMX21348
• Remove insert to fit most single lever cartridges with square broaches

Item #	Length (in)
ABRMX34103	3 ¼

To Order Call: 1.800.767.5552 . Fax: 1.800.886.9831

*Original Mfg's names are used for identification only and are not a representation that the items offered are genuine items of the original Mfg.

Quality Replacement Parts

BRASS AMERICA
Quality Replacement Parts

Drinking Fountain Parts

HAWS*
Bubbler Head
Drinking Fountain

- Solid brass
- Chrome finish

Item #	IPS Inlet (in)
ABRCBF360-LF	⅜

ELKAY*
Metal Cartridge
Drinking Fountain

- Fits various manufacturers

Item #
ABRCBF360-3-LF

IMPORT
Plastic Cartridge
Drinking Fountain

- Fits various manufacturers

Item #
ABRCBF360-3-P

Bubbler Head
Drinking Fountain
W/ Flange & Shank

Item #
ABRCBF360-KIT-LF

Drinking Fountain Valve Retro Kit w/o Cartridge

- Push activated, labeled "IN" & "OUT" for supply line placement
- Replaces OEM housing & retainer nut

Item #
LF124620

Drinking Fountain Valve Retro Kit with Cartridge

- Push activated, labeled "IN" & "OUT" for supply line placement
- Replaces OEM#: Haws: 5874SS Acorn: 7000-050-001 & Others

Item #
LF124640

Faucet Repair Parts

Cartridge
Plastic

Item #	Length (in)	Broach	H/C	Color
ABRCTG-LEV-HOT	2	"D"	H	Red
ABRCTG-LEV-COLD	2	"D"	C	White

Diverter Stem
Plastic

- Fits Premier
- See ABR1300DIVBOOT for mating part

Item #	Length (in)	Broach
ABR1300DIV	3 ¼	"D"

PREMIER*
Replacement Boot
Rubber

- See ABR1300DIV for mating part

Item #
ABR1300DIVBOOT

Aerator
Male

Item #	Size (in)	Finish
ABRPBAERATOR-LF	¹⁵⁄₁₆	Polished Brass
ABRCPAERATOR-LF	¹⁵⁄₁₆	Chrome

Spray Hose Escutcheon
Kitchen

Item #
ABRSPRAY-ESC

Spray Hose
Kitchen

- Hose only

Item #	Length (in)
ABRSPRAY-HOSE	48

Spray Nozzle
Kitchen

Item #
ABRSPRAY-NOZZLE

Supply Stops

Supply Stop
1/4 Turn, Straight

Item #	Inlet/FIP (in)	Outlet/Comp (in)
ABRBV12F38CS-LF	½	⅜

To Order Call: 1.800.767.5552 . Fax: 1.800.886.9831

Original Mfg's names are used for identification only and are not a representation that the items offered are genuine items of the original Mfg.

37

Quality Replacement Parts

Supply Stop
1/4 Turn,
Straight

Item #	Inlet/FIP (in)	Outlet/ Comp (in)
ABRBV12F38CS	½	⅜
ABRBV12F12CS	½	½

Supply Stop
1/4 Turn,
Straight

NSF / ANSI 372
Compliant

Item #	Inlet/ Comp (in)	Outlet/ Comp (in)
ABRBV58C38CS-LF	⅝	⅜
ABRBV58C12CS-LF	⅝	½

Supply Stop
1/4 Turn,
Straight

Item #	Inlet/ Comp (in)	Outlet/ Comp (in)
ABRBV58C38CS	⅝	⅜
ABRBV58C12CS	⅝	½

Supply Stop
1/4 Turn,
Angle

NSF / ANSI 372
Compliant

Item #	Inlet/ Comp (in)	Outlet/ Comp (in)
ABRBV58C38CA-LF	⅝	⅜

Supply Stop
1/4 Turn,
Angle

Item #	Inlet/ Comp (in)	Outlet/ Comp (in)
ABRBV58C12CA	⅝	½

Supply Stop
1/4 Turn,
Angle

NSF / ANSI 372
Compliant

Item #	Inlet/FIP (in)	Outlet/ Comp (in)
ABRBV12F38CA-LF	½	⅜

Supply Stop
1/4 Turn,
Angle

Item #	Inlet/FIP (in)	Outlet/ Comp (in)
ABRBV12F12CA	½	½

Supply Stop
Compression,
Straight

NSF / ANSI 372
Compliant

Item #	Inlet/ Comp (in)	Outlet/ Comp (in)
ABR58C38CS-LF	⅝	⅜
ABR38C38CS-LF	⅜	⅜

Supply Stop
Compression,
Straight

Item #	Inlet/ Comp (in)	Outlet/ Comp (in)
ABR58C38CS	⅝	⅜
ABR12C12CS	½	½

Supply Stop
FIP x
Compression,
Straight

Item #	Inlet (in)	Outlet/ Comp (in)
ABR12F12CS	½	½
ABR12F38CS	½	⅜

Supply Stop
Comp x FIP,
Straight

NSF / ANSI 372
Compliant

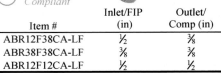

Item #	Inlet/FIP (in)	Outlet/ Comp (in)
ABR12F38CA-LF	½	⅜
ABR38F38CA-LF	⅜	⅜
ABR12F12CA-LF	½	½

Supply Stop
Compression,
Angle

NSF / ANSI 372
Compliant

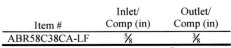

Item #	Inlet/ Comp (in)	Outlet/ Comp (in)
ABR58C38CA-LF	⅝	⅜

Supply Stop
Compression,
Angle

Item #	Inlet/ Comp (in)	Outlet/ Comp (in)
ABR58C38CA	⅝	⅜
ABR58C12CA	⅝	½

Tub & Shower

Diverter
Gate
Plastic

• Chrome knob

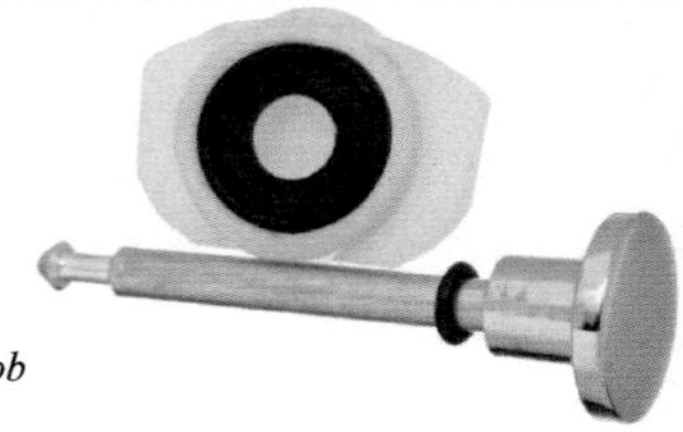

Item #
ABRAB1200

Tub
Spout
Chrome
Plated Zinc

Item #	Size (in)
ABRAB1201	½" FIP Front

Diverter Spout
Chrome Plated Zinc

Item #	Size (in)
ABRAB1211	½" FIP Front

Diverter Spout
Chrome Plated Zinc

Item #	Size (in)
ABRAB1213	½ or ¾ Adjustable

Diverter Spout
Chrome Plated Zinc

Item #	Size (in)
ABRAB1221	½ or ¾ Adjustable

Diverter Spout
Chrome Plated Zinc

• *Includes male adapter*

Item #	Size (in)
ABRAB1224	½ or ¾ Adjustable

Diverter Spout
Chrome Plated Zinc

• *Includes female adapter*

Item #	Size (in)
ABRAB1225	½ or ¾ Adjustable

Tub Spout
Chrome Plated Zinc

• *Slip-fit*
• *Includes set screw*

Item #	Description
ABRAB1230	Clamps over ½" copper

Diverter Spout
Chrome Plated Zinc

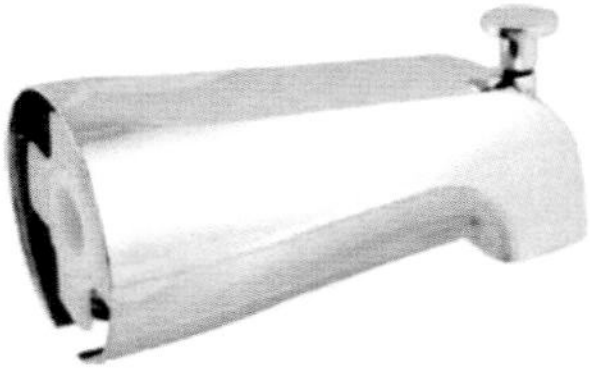

• *Includes slip connect for copper and set screw*

Item #	Size (in)
ABRAB1231	½" Front

Diverter Spout
Chrome Plated Zinc

• *Includes male adapter*

Item #	Description
ABRAB1240	½ & ¾ Wall End

Tub Spout
Chrome Plated Zinc

• *Adjustable to 2"*

Item #	Description
ABRAB1243	Clamps over ½" copper

Tub Spout
Chrome Plated Zinc

Item #	Size (in)
ABRAB1245	½ & ¾ IPS Front

Diverter Spout
Chrome

Item #	Size (in)
ABRAB1250	½ & ¾ Wall End

Face Plate
Chrome

Item #	Description
ABRAB5120	Face Plate & Screws
ABRSCP5120	1 ½" Screws

Tub Trip Lever
Chrome

• *Includes two screws*

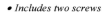

Item #
ABRAB5130

Lift & Turn Drain
Chrome

Item #	O.D. (in)	Thread
ABRAB5211	1.50	Coarse

Lift & Turn Drain
Chrome

Item #	O.D. (in)	Thread
ABRAB5213	1.63	Fine

To Order Call: 1.800.767.5552 . Fax: 1.800.886.9831

Original Mfg's names are used for identification only and are not a representation that the items offered are genuine items of the original Mfg.

39

Quality Replacement Parts

Tip Toe Cartridge
Plastic

• Chrome top

Item #	O.D. (in)	Thread
ABRAB5221-CTG	0.94	18 TPI
ABRAB5222-CTG	0.38	18 TPI

Shower Head
Chrome

• With brass ball

Item #	GPM
ABRSC6400	2.5

NIAGARA*
Shower Head
Acrylic

• With brass ball
• Adjustable

Item #	GPM
ABRSC6401	2.5

Shower Head
Chrome

Item #	Face (dia.)
ABRSC6421	1.50

Shower Head
Chrome

• With brass ball

Item #	Face (dia.)
ABRSC6425	1.75

Shower Arm
Chrome

Item #	Length (in)
ABRSHOWER-ARM	6.00
ABRSHOWER-ARM-8	8.00

Swivel Connector
Chrome

Item #
ABR3003

Slip Joint Nut
Chrome Plated Zinc

Item #	Dia. (in)
ABRAB6011Z-1	1 ¼ x 1 ¼
ABRAB6011Z-2	1 ½ x 1 ¼
ABRAB6011Z-3	1 ½ x 1 ½

Test Plug

Item #	Size (in)
ABRAB038-2	2
ABRAB038-3	3
ABRAB038-4	4

Toilet & Urinal Parts

Flush Handle
Brass Arm

• Zinc nut

Item #	Length (in)
ABRAB0502	8

Flush Handle
Brass Arm

• Metal Lock Washer
• Premium tank lever
• New enlarged brass nut
• New fiber impregnated rubber washer

Item #
ABRCPI0503NS

Flush Handle
Brass Arm

• Offset flat arm

Item #	Length (in)
ABRAB0511	10

KOHLER*
Flush Handle
Brass Arm

Item #	Length (in)
ABRAB0517	8

ELJER*
Flush Handle
Brass Arm

Item #	Length (in)
ABRAB0534	9 ¼

KOHLER*
Flush Handle
Plastic Arm

Item #	Length (in)
ABRAB0541	8 ½

To Order Call: 1.800.767.5552 . Fax: 1.800.886.9831

40   *Original Mfg's names are used for identification only and are not a representation that the items offered are genuine items of the original Mfg.*

ABRASS
AMERICA
Quality Replacement Parts

Flush Handle
Plastic

- Eljer style touch flush

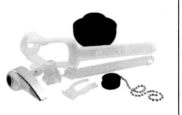

Item #
ABRAB6201

Flapper
Rubber
Kohler Style

Item #
ABRAB191006

Flapper
Rubber
Korky Style

- Universal

Item #
ABRAB2035

Flapper
Rubber

- With styrofome
- Crane old style #57

Item #
ABRAB2055

COAST*
Toilet Flapper
Vinyl
Old Style

- Universal

Item #
ABRAB32079-B

COAST*
Toilet Flapper
Vinyl
New Style

- Universal

Item #
ABRAB32080-B

Seat Bolts
Plastic

Item #	Size (mm)
ABRAB57130	11
ABRAB57160	9

Flapper Box

Item #
ABRFLAPBOX

Urinal Spud

Item #	Size (in)
ABRCS100X075	1 x ¾

Closet Spud

Item #	Size (in)
ABRCS125	1 ¼

Closet Spud

Item #	Size (in)
ABRCS150	1 ½

Closet Spud

Item #	Size (in)
ABRCS200	2

Closet Spud

Item #	Size (in)
ABRCS200X125	2 x 1 ¼

Closet Spud

Item #	Size (in)
ABRCS200X150	2 x 1 ½

Send Your ABRASS Orders To:

BARRY E. | WALTER | SR. CO.

Fax or E-mail:
orderdesk@barrywalter.com

To Order Call: 1.800.767.5552 . Fax: 1.800.886.9831

Original Mfg's names are used for identification only and are not a representation that the items offered are genuine items of the original Mfg.

41

Quality Replacement Parts

Quality Replacement Parts

Replacement Parts

Bibb Washers
Flat

Item #	Size (in)
ABRAB9605	1/4S-00
ABRAB9615	1/4M-0
ABRAB9635	1/4R
ABRAB9655	1/4L
ABRAB9675	3/8R
ABRAB9695	3/8M
ABRAB9705	3/8L
ABRAB9725	1/2M

Bibb Washers
Beveled

Item #	Size (in)
ABRAB9805	1/4S-00
ABRAB9815	1/4M-0
ABRAB9835	1/4R
ABRAB9855	1/4L
ABRAB9875	3/8R
ABRAB9895	3/8M
ABRAB9905	3/8L
ABRAB9925	1/2R

Sponge Overflow Washer
Beveled

Item #	Size (in)
ABRAB1308L	3.25 x 2.25 x 0.19

Stopper
Rubber
- Universal
- For sinks & tubs

Item #	Size (in)
ABRAB133	.038 - 1.00
ABRAB135	1.50 - 2.00

Stopper
Flat

Item #	Size (in)
ABRAB134	5.00

Stopper
Disposal

Item #	Size (in)
ABRAB5110	4.00

Disposal Drain Seal
Rubber Hush Cushion

Item #
ABRAB303

AMERICAN STANDARD*
Flush Valve Seal
Rubber

Item #
ABRAB40413

AMERICAN STANDARD*
Tank to Bowl Gasket
Sponge
- Close couple

Item #
ABRAB40491

AMERICAN STANDARD*
Disk
Snap On

Item #
ABRAB453A

AMERICAN STANDARD*
Disk
Screw On

Item #
ABRAB7523

Poly Washers
Slip Joint & Tail Piece

Item #	Size (in)	Type	Color
ABRSPM-100	1.50	Slip Joint	Black
ABRSPM-200	1.25	Slip Joint	White
ABRTP-8120-C	1.50	Tail Piece	Clear

Tools

Broach Gauge
Plastic
- Identifies make of stem
- 34 broach sizes

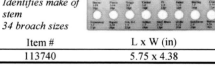

Item #	L x W (in)
113740	5.75 x 4.38

Send Your ABRASS Orders To:

BARRY E. WALTER SR. CO.

Fax or E-mail:
orderdesk@barrywalter.com

To Order Call: 1.800.767.5552 . Fax: 1.800.886.9831

42 *Original Mfg's names are used for identification only and are not a representation that the items offered are genuine items of the original Mfg.

To Order Call: 1.800.767.5552 . Fax: 1.800.886.9831

42 *Original Mfg's names are used for identification only and are not a representation that the items offered are genuine items of the original Mfg.
To Order Call: 1.800.767.5552 . Fax: 1.800.886.9831

42 *Original Mfg's names are used for identification only and are not a representation that the items offered are genuine items of the original Mfg.

Quality Replacement Parts

Binford Faucets

Lavatory Faucet
Washerless, Two Handle
• Chrome plated brass

Item #	Pop-Up
ABF1010-LF	W/ ABS
ABF1010LP-LF	Less

Lavatory Faucet
Washerless, ADA Two Handle
• Chrome plated brass

Item #	Pop-Up
ABF2510DHLP-LF	Less

Lavatory Faucet
Washerless, Single Handle
• Chrome plated brass

Item #	Pop-Up
ABF5510	W/ ABS

Lavatory Faucet
Washerless, Single Handle

Item #	Pop-Up	Finish
ABF5510LSB-LF	W/ Brass	Chrome
ABF5510LSLP-LF	Less	Chrome
ABF5510LSBSN-LF	W/ Brass	Nickel

Kitchen Faucet
Washerless, Two Handle
• Chrome plated brass

Item #	Spray
ABF1210-LF	Less
ABF1220-LF	With

Spray Diverter
Plastic

• Fits Jameco
• Fits Binford 1220 faucet

Item #
ABR1220DIV-LF

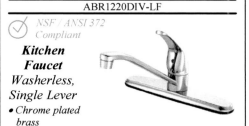

Kitchen Faucet
Washerless, Single Lever
• Chrome plated brass

Item #	Spray
ABF5710LS-LF	Less
ABF5720LS-LF	With

Spray Diverter
Plastic

• Fits Binford 5720 faucet

Item #
ABR5720DIV-LF

Tub & Shower Faucet
Washerless, Single Lever
• Chrome plated brass

Item #
ABF5310LS

Tub & Shower Faucet
Pressure Balancing, Single Lever
• Chrome plated brass
• Anti-Scald
• Integral stops

Item #
ABF5371L

Tub & Shower Faucet
Washerless, Two Handle
• Chrome plated brass

Item #
ABF1410

Sleeve
Chrome

• Fits ABF1410 faucet

Item #	Length (in)	O.D. (in)	Thread
ABRSLEEVE-1410	2 23/32	1	1"-24

Service Sink Faucet
Two Handle Wall Mount
• Satin chrome plated brass
• 6-1/2" spout w/ vaccum breakers

Item #
ABF3050-LF

Service Sink Faucet
Two Handle Wall Mount
• Satin chrome plated brass
• 2-1/2" spout w/ vaccum breakers

Item #
ABF3055-LF

Wall Mount Faucet
Two Handle
• Chrome plated brass
• Gooseneck spout
• 4" centers

Item #
ABF3057-LF

To Order Call: 1.800.767.5552 . Fax: 1.800.886.9831

Original Mfg's names are used for identification only and are not a representation that the items offered are genuine items of the original Mfg.

NSF / ANSI 372 Compliant

Wall Mount Faucet
Two Handle
- Chrome plated brass
- Adjustable centers

Item #	Spout Size (in)
ABF3059-LF	8
ABF3060-LF	12
ABF3061-LF	18

NSF / ANSI 372 Compliant

Faucet Spout
Chrome

Item #	Spout Size (in)
ABF3059-SPOUT-LF	8
ABF3060-SPOUT-LF	12
ABF3061-SPOUT-LF	18

NSF / ANSI 372 Compliant

Heavy Deck Mount Faucet
Two Handle
- Chrome plated brass
- Gooseneck spout
- 4" centers

Item #
ABF3104-LF

NSF / ANSI 372 Compliant

Heavy Deck Mount Faucet
Two Handle
- Chrome plated brass
- 6" spout
- 4" centers

Item #
ABF3105-LF

NSF / ANSI 372 Compliant

Deck Mount Pantry Faucet
Two Handle
- Chrome plated brass
- 10" Gooseneck spout

Item #
ABF3111-LF

NSF / ANSI 372 Compliant

Pre-Rinse Unit
Deck Mount
- Chrome plated brass
- Adjustable 7-1/2" to 8-1/2" centers

Item #
ABF3612-LF

NSF / ANSI 372 Compliant

Pre-Rinse Unit
Wall Mount
- Chrome plated brass
- Adjustable 7-1/2" to 8-1/2" centers

Item #
ABF3013-LF

NSF / ANSI 372 Compliant

Single Basin Cock
Compression, Single Handle
- Chrome plated brass
- Each includes "H" & "C" buttons

Item #
ABFSBC-LF

PHOENIX*
Tub & Shower Faucet
Washerless, Two Handle

Item #
ABF4812

Faucet Drains & Pop-Ups

Pop-Up Assembly
Brass

Item #	Finish
ABRBP-10	Chrome
ABRBP-10-PVD	PVD Coated

Grid Drain
Brass
- Chrome plated

Item #	L x W (in)
ABRGD-10	8 x 1 1/4

ADA Grid Drain
Brass
- Chrome plated

Item #	Length (in)
ABRGD-10H	8

Pop-Up Assembly
Plastic
- Chrome plated top

Item #
ABRPP-01

Pop-Up Plug
Plastic
For Price Pfister
- Chrome plated brass top

Item #
ABRAB1165

Pop-Up Stopper
Plastic
For Delta/Universal
- Chrome plated top

Item #
ABRDL9200PCP

To Order Call: 1.800.767.5552 . Fax: 1.800.886.9831

44   *Original Mfg's names are used for identification only and are not a representation that the items offered are genuine items of the original Mfg.*

Quality Replacement Parts

AMERICAN BRASS*
2-Valve Rebuild Kit

AMERICAN BRASS*
3-Valve Rebuild Kit

AMERICAN BRASS*
2-Valve Rebuild Kit

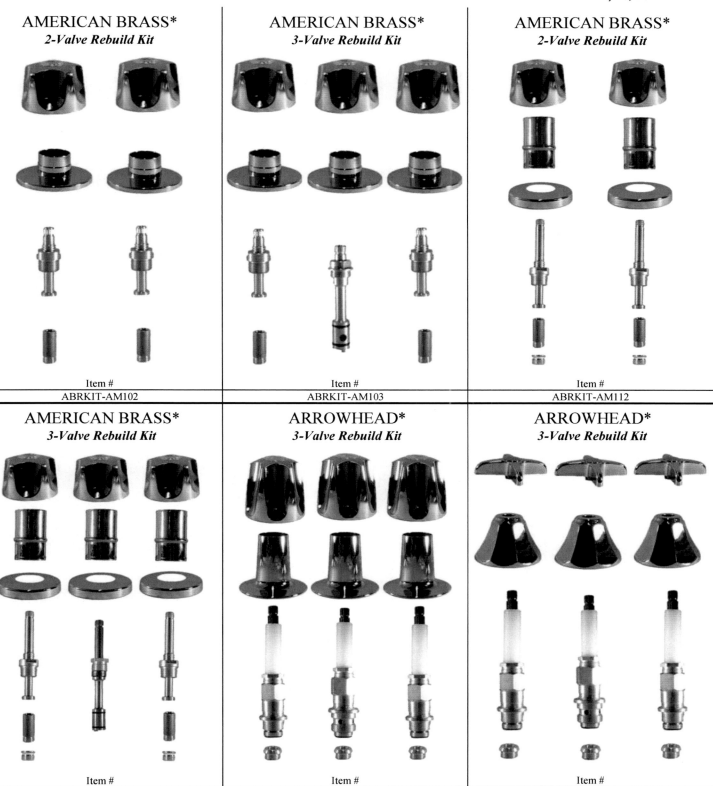

Item #
ABRKIT-AM102

Item #
ABRKIT-AM103

Item #
ABRKIT-AM112

AMERICAN BRASS*
3-Valve Rebuild Kit

ARROWHEAD*
3-Valve Rebuild Kit

ARROWHEAD*
3-Valve Rebuild Kit

Item #
ABRKIT-AM113

Item #
ABRKIT-AR103

Item #
ABRKIT-AR113

To Order Call: 1.800.767.5552 . Fax: 1.800.886.9831

Quality Replacement Parts

AMERICAN STANDARD* *2-Valve Rebuild Kit*	AMERICAN STANDARD* *3-Valve Rebuild Kit*	AMERICAN STANDARD* *2-Valve Rebuild Kit*
Item # ABRKIT-AS102	Item # ABRKIT-AS103	Item # ABRKIT-AS112
AMERICAN STANDARD* *3-Valve Rebuild Kit*	AMERICAN STANDARD* *2-Valve Rebuild Kit*	AMERICAN STANDARD* *3-Valve Rebuild Kit*
Item # ABRKIT-AS113	Item # ABRKIT-AS122	Item # ABRKIT-AS123

To Order Call: 1.800.767.5552 . Fax: 1.800.886.9831

Original Mfg's names are used for identification only and are not a representation that the items offered are genuine items of the original Mfg.

AMERICAN STANDARD*	AMERICAN STANDARD*	AMERICAN STANDARD*
2-Valve Rebuild Kit	*3-Valve Rebuild Kit*	*2-Valve Rebuild Kit*
Item #	Item #	Item #
ABRKIT-AS132	ABRKIT-AS133	ABRKIT-AS142
AMERICAN STANDARD*	AMERICAN STANDARD*	AMERICAN STANDARD*
3-Valve Rebuild Kit	*3-Valve Rebuild Kit*	*2-Valve Rebuild Kit*
Item #	Item #	Item #
ABRKIT-AS143	ABRKIT-AS153	ABRKIT-AS162

To Order Call: 1.800.767.5552 . Fax: 1.800.886.9831

Quality Replacement Parts

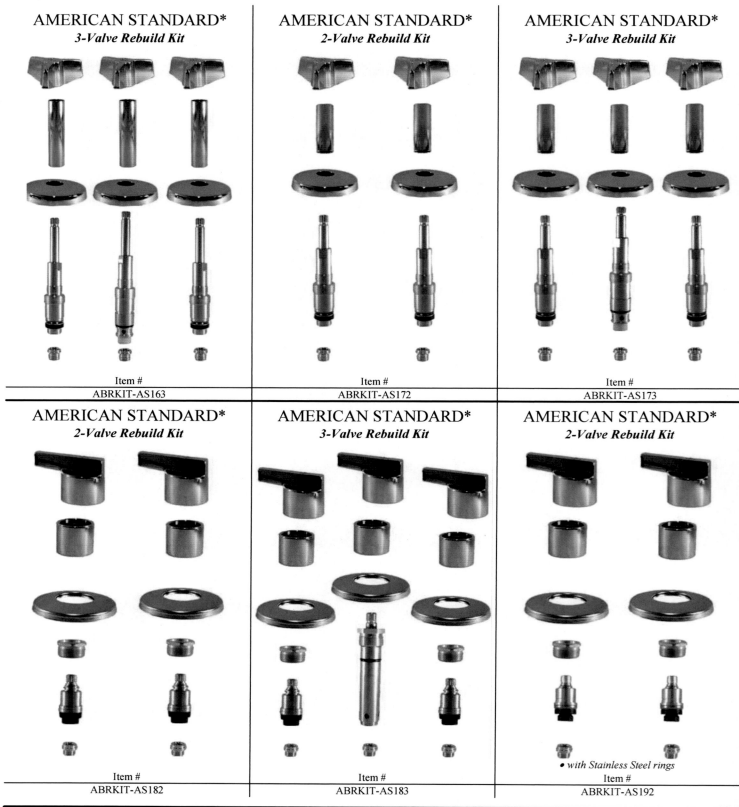

AMERICAN STANDARD*	AMERICAN STANDARD*	AMERICAN STANDARD*
3-Valve Rebuild Kit	*2-Valve Rebuild Kit*	*3-Valve Rebuild Kit*
Item #	Item #	Item #
ABRKIT-AS163	ABRKIT-AS172	ABRKIT-AS173
AMERICAN STANDARD*	AMERICAN STANDARD*	AMERICAN STANDARD*
2-Valve Rebuild Kit	*3-Valve Rebuild Kit*	*2-Valve Rebuild Kit*
		• with Stainless Steel rings
Item #	Item #	Item #
ABRKIT-AS182	ABRKIT-AS183	ABRKIT-AS192

To Order Call: 1.800.767.5552 . Fax: 1.800.886.9831

Original Mfg's names are used for identification only and are not a representation that the items offered are genuine items of the original Mfg.

Quality Replacement Parts

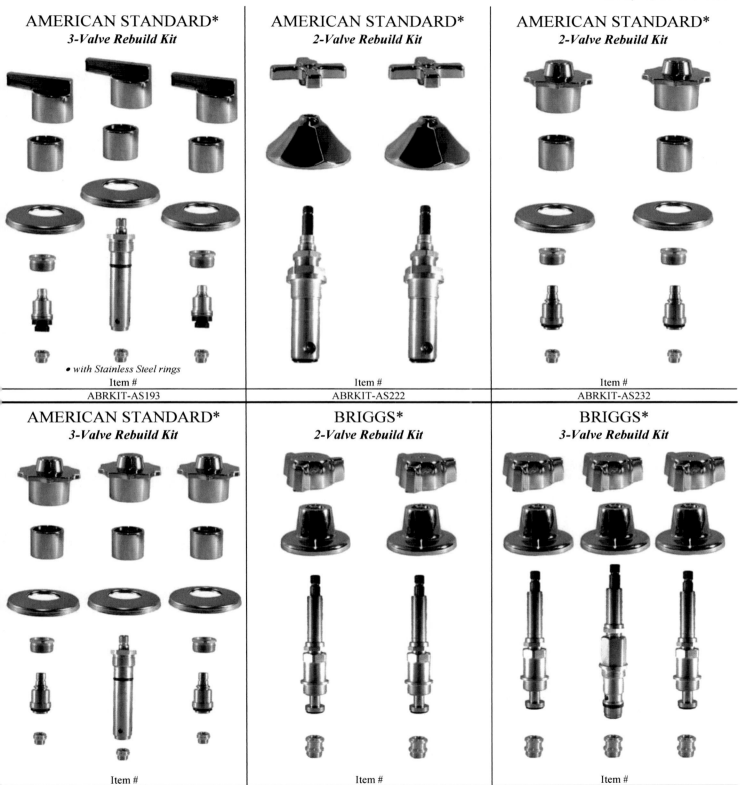

AMERICAN STANDARD*
3-Valve Rebuild Kit

• with Stainless Steel rings
Item #
ABRKIT-AS193

AMERICAN STANDARD*
2-Valve Rebuild Kit

Item #
ABRKIT-AS222

AMERICAN STANDARD*
2-Valve Rebuild Kit

Item #
ABRKIT-AS232

AMERICAN STANDARD*
3-Valve Rebuild Kit

Item #
ABRKIT-AS233

BRIGGS*
2-Valve Rebuild Kit

Item #
ABRKIT-BR102

BRIGGS*
3-Valve Rebuild Kit

Item #
ABRKIT-BR103

To Order Call: 1.800.767.5552 . Fax: 1.800.886.9831

Original Mfg's names are used for identification only and are not a representation that the items offered are genuine items of the original Mfg.

49

Quality Replacement Parts

BRIGGS*
3-Valve Rebuild Kit

Item #
ABRKIT-BR113

BRIGGS*
2-Valve Rebuild Kit

Item #
ABRKIT-BR122

BRIGGS*
3-Valve Rebuild Kit

Item #
ABRKIT-BR123

CENTRAL BRASS*
2-Valve Rebuild Kit

Item #
ABRKIT-CB102

CENTRAL BRASS*
3-Valve Rebuild Kit

Item #
ABRKIT-CB103

CENTRAL BRASS*
2-Valve Rebuild Kit

Item #
ABRKIT-CB112

To Order Call: 1.800.767.5552 . Fax: 1.800.886.9831

Original Mfg's names are used for identification only and are not a representation that the items offered are genuine items of the original Mfg.

Quality Replacement Parts

CENTRAL BRASS* *3-Valve Rebuild Kit*	CENTRAL BRASS* *2-Valve Rebuild Kit*	CENTRAL BRASS* *3-Valve Rebuild Kit*
Item # ABRKIT-CB113	Item # ABRKIT-CB122	Item # ABRKIT-CB123
CENTRAL BRASS* *2-Valve Rebuild Kit*	CENTRAL BRASS* *3-Valve Rebuild Kit*	CENTRAL BRASS* *2-Valve Rebuild Kit*
Item # ABRKIT-CB132	Item # ABRKIT-CB133	Item # ABRKIT-CB142

To Order Call: 1.800.767.5552 . Fax: 1.800.886.9831

*Original Mfg's names are used for identification only and are not a representation that the items offered are genuine items of the original Mfg.

51

Quality Replacement Parts

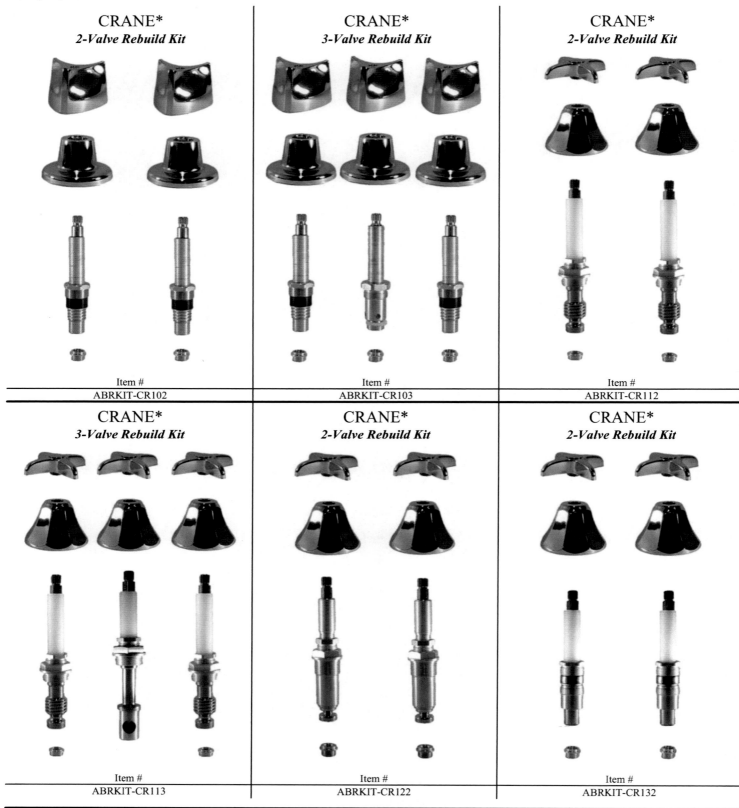

CRANE*
2-Valve Rebuild Kit

Item #
ABRKIT-CR102

CRANE*
3-Valve Rebuild Kit

Item #
ABRKIT-CR103

CRANE*
2-Valve Rebuild Kit

Item #
ABRKIT-CR112

CRANE*
3-Valve Rebuild Kit

Item #
ABRKIT-CR113

CRANE*
2-Valve Rebuild Kit

Item #
ABRKIT-CR122

CRANE*
2-Valve Rebuild Kit

Item #
ABRKIT-CR132

To Order Call: 1.800.767.5552 . Fax: 1.800.886.9831

Original Mfg's names are used for identification only and are not a representation that the items offered are genuine items of the original Mfg.

Quality Replacement Parts

CRANE* *3-Valve Rebuild Kit*	CRANE* *2-Valve Rebuild Kit*	CRANE* *2-Valve Rebuild Kit*
Item # ABRKIT-CR133	Item # ABRKIT-CR142	Item # ABRKIT-CR152
CRANE* *3-Valve Rebuild Kit*	ELJER* *2-Valve Rebuild Kit*	ELJER* *3-Valve Rebuild Kit*
Item # ABRKIT-CR153	Item # ABRKIT-EL102	Item # ABRKIT-EL103

To Order Call: 1.800.767.5552 . Fax: 1.800.886.9831

Original Mfg's names are used for identification only and are not a representation that the items offered are genuine items of the original Mfg.

Quality Replacement Parts

ELJER*
2-Valve Rebuild Kit

Item #
ABRKIT-EL112

ELJER*
3-Valve Rebuild Kit

Item #
ABRKIT-EL113

ELJER*
3-Valve Rebuild Kit

Item #
ABRKIT-EL123

ELJER*
2-Valve Rebuild Kit

Item #
ABRKIT-EL132

ELJER*
3-Valve Rebuild Kit

Item #
ABRKIT-EL133

ELJER*
3-Valve Rebuild Kit

Item #
ABRKIT-EL143

To Order Call: 1.800.767.5552 . Fax: 1.800.886.9831

Original Mfg's names are used for identification only and are not a representation that the items offered are genuine items of the original Mfg.

BRASS AMERICA
Quality Replacement Parts

ELJER*	ELJER*	GERBER*
2-Valve Rebuild Kit	*3-Valve Rebuild Kit*	*2-Valve Rebuild Kit*
Item #	Item #	Item #
ABRKIT-EL152	ABRKIT-EL153	ABRKIT-GE102
GERBER*	GERBER*	GERBER*
3-Valve Rebuild Kit	*2-Valve Rebuild Kit*	*3-Valve Rebuild Kit*
Item #	Item #	Item #
ABRKIT-GE103	ABRKIT-GE112	ABRKIT-GE113

Quality Replacement Parts

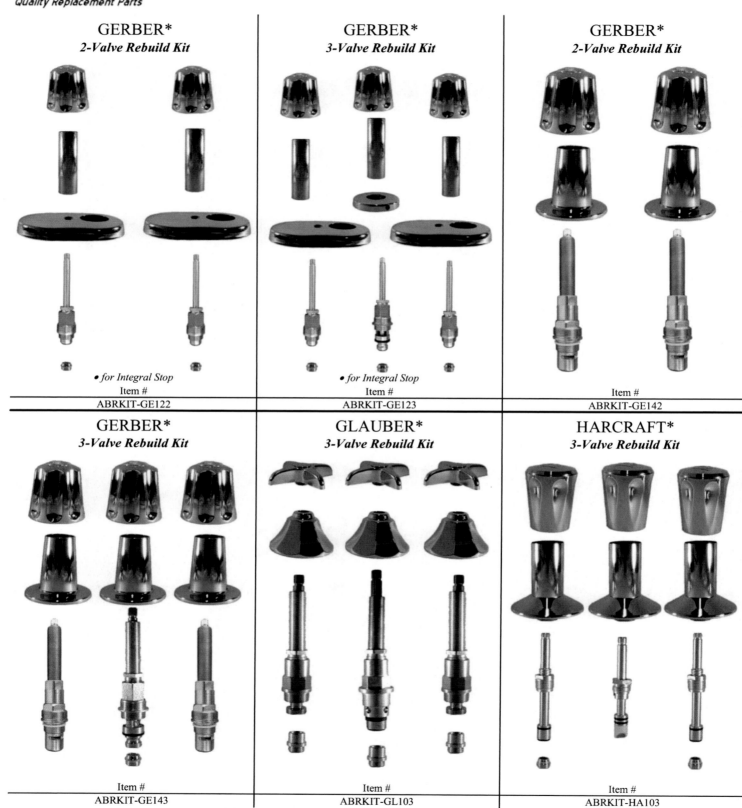

GERBER*
2-Valve Rebuild Kit

• *for Integral Stop*

Item #
ABRKIT-GE122

GERBER*
3-Valve Rebuild Kit

• *for Integral Stop*

Item #
ABRKIT-GE123

GERBER*
2-Valve Rebuild Kit

Item #
ABRKIT-GE142

GERBER*
3-Valve Rebuild Kit

Item #
ABRKIT-GE143

GLAUBER*
3-Valve Rebuild Kit

Item #
ABRKIT-GL103

HARCRAFT*
3-Valve Rebuild Kit

Item #
ABRKIT-HA103

To Order Call: 1.800.767.5552 . Fax: 1.800.886.9831

Original Mfg's names are used for identification only and are not a representation that the items offered are genuine items of the original Mfg.

Quality Replacement Parts

BRASS AMERICA
Quality Replacement Parts

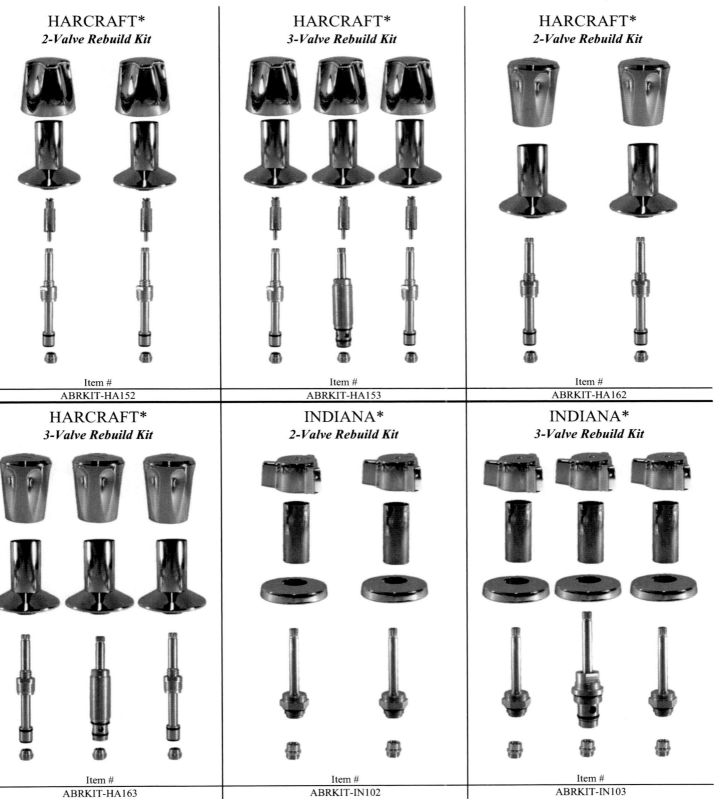

HARCRAFT* 2-Valve Rebuild Kit	HARCRAFT* 3-Valve Rebuild Kit	HARCRAFT* 2-Valve Rebuild Kit
Item # ABRKIT-HA152	Item # ABRKIT-HA153	Item # ABRKIT-HA162
HARCRAFT* 3-Valve Rebuild Kit	**INDIANA*** 2-Valve Rebuild Kit	**INDIANA*** 3-Valve Rebuild Kit
Item # ABRKIT-HA163	Item # ABRKIT-IN102	Item # ABRKIT-IN103

To Order Call: 1.800.767.5552 . Fax: 1.800.886.9831

Original Mfg's names are used for identification only and are not a representation that the items offered are genuine items of the original Mfg. **57**

Quality Replacement Parts

INDIANA*
3-Valve Rebuild Kit

Item #
ABRKIT-IN113

KOHLER*
2-Valve Rebuild Kit

Item #
ABRKIT-KO102

KOHLER*
3-Valve Rebuild Kit

Item #
ABRKIT-KO103

KOHLER*
2-Valve Rebuild Kit

Item #
ABRKIT-KO112

KOHLER*
3-Valve Rebuild Kit

Item #
ABRKIT-KO113

KOHLER*
2-Valve Rebuild Kit

Item #
ABRKIT-KO122

To Order Call: 1.800.767.5552 . Fax: 1.800.886.9831

*Original Mfg's names are used for identification only and are not a representation that the items offered are genuine items of the original Mfg.

Quality Replacement Parts

BRASS AMERICA
Quality Replacement Parts

KOHLER*
3-Valve Rebuild Kit

Item #
ABRKIT-KO123

KOHLER*
2-Valve Rebuild Kit

Item #
ABRKIT-KO132

KOHLER*
3-Valve Rebuild Kit

Item #
ABRKIT-KO133

KOHLER*
3-Valve Rebuild Kit

Item #
ABRKIT-KO143

KOHLER*
2-Valve Rebuild Kit

Item #
ABRKIT-KO152

KOHLER*
3-Valve Rebuild Kit

Item #
ABRKIT-KO153

To Order Call: 1.800.767.5552 . Fax: 1.800.886.9831

*Original Mfg's names are used for identification only and are not a representation that the items offered are genuine items of the original Mfg.

Quality Replacement Parts

KOHLER*
2-Valve Rebuild Kit

Item #
ABRKIT-KO162

KOHLER*
3-Valve Rebuild Kit

Item #
ABRKIT-KO163

KOHLER*
2-Valve Rebuild Kit

Item #
ABRKIT-KO172

KOHLER*
3-Valve Rebuild Kit

Item #
ABRKIT-KO183

MIXET*
Single Handle Rebuild Kit

Item #
ABRKIT-MX101

NIBCO*
Single Handle Rebuild Kit

Item #
ABRKIT-NI101

To Order Call: 1.800.767.5552 . Fax: 1.800.886.9831

Original Mfg's names are used for identification only and are not a representation that the items offered are genuine items of the original Mfg.

Quality Replacement Parts

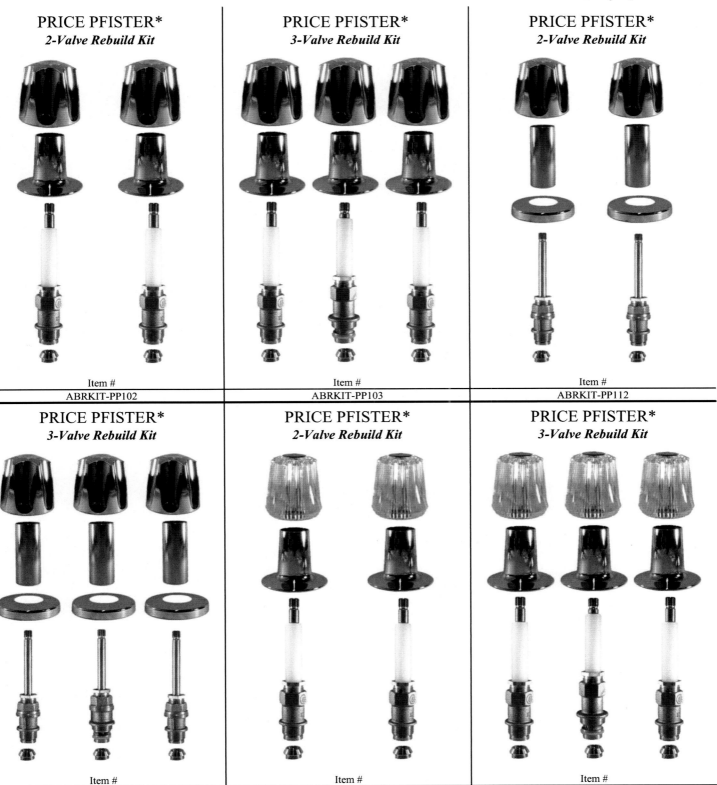

PRICE PFISTER* 2-Valve Rebuild Kit	PRICE PFISTER* 3-Valve Rebuild Kit	PRICE PFISTER* 2-Valve Rebuild Kit
Item # ABRKIT-PP102	Item # ABRKIT-PP103	Item # ABRKIT-PP112
PRICE PFISTER* 3-Valve Rebuild Kit	**PRICE PFISTER*** 2-Valve Rebuild Kit	**PRICE PFISTER*** 3-Valve Rebuild Kit
Item # ABRKIT-PP113	Item # ABRKIT-PP122	Item # ABRKIT-PP123

To Order Call: 1.800.767.5552 . Fax: 1.800.886.9831

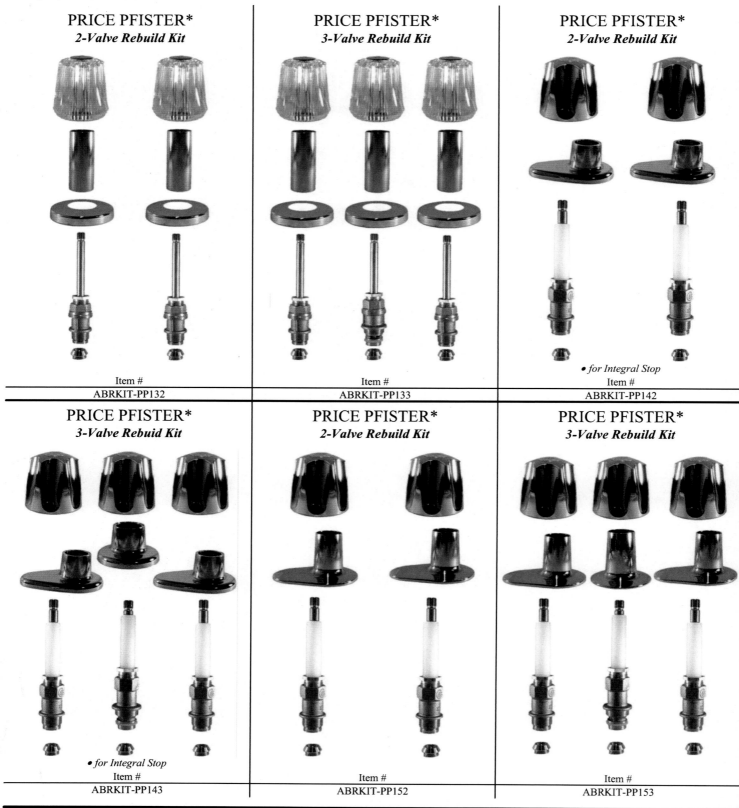

PRICE PFISTER*
2-Valve Rebuild Kit

Item #
ABRKIT-PP132

PRICE PFISTER*
3-Valve Rebuild Kit

Item #
ABRKIT-PP133

PRICE PFISTER*
2-Valve Rebuild Kit

• *for Integral Stop*
Item #
ABRKIT-PP142

PRICE PFISTER*
3-Valve Rebuid Kit

• *for Integral Stop*
Item #
ABRKIT-PP143

PRICE PFISTER*
2-Valve Rebuild Kit

Item #
ABRKIT-PP152

PRICE PFISTER*
3-Valve Rebuild Kit

Item #
ABRKIT-PP153

To Order Call: 1.800.767.5552 . Fax: 1.800.886.9831

62   *Original Mfg's names are used for identification only and are not a representation that the items offered are genuine items of the original Mfg.*

PRICE PFISTER*
2-Valve Rebuild Kit

Item #
ABRKIT-PP162

PRICE PFISTER*
3-Valve Rebuild Kit

Item #
ABRKIT-PP163

PRICE PFISTER*
2-Valve Rebuild Kit

Item #
ABRKIT-PP172

PRICE PFISTER*
3-Valve Rebuid Kit

Item #
ABRKIT-PP173

PRICE PFISTER*
2-Valve Rebuild Kit

Item #
ABRKIT-PP182

PRICE PFISTER*
3-Valve Rebuild Kit

Item #
ABRKIT-PP183

To Order Call: 1.800.767.5552 . Fax: 1.800.886.9831

Original Mfg's names are used for identification only and are not a representation that the items offered are genuine items of the original Mfg.

Quality Replacement Parts

PRICE PFISTER*
3-Valve Rebuild Kit

Item #
ABRKIT-PP193

ROYAL BRASS*
2-Valve Rebuild Kit

Item #
ABRKIT-RY102

SAYCO*
2-Valve Rebuild Kit

Item #
ABRKIT-SA102

SAYCO*
3-Valve Rebuild Kit

Item #
ABRKIT-SA103

SAYCO*
3-Valve Rebuild Kit

Item #
ABRKIT-SA113

SAYCO*
2-Valve Rebuild Kit

Item #
ABRKIT-SA132

To Order Call: 1.800.767.5552 . Fax: 1.800.886.9831

*Original Mfg's names are used for identification only and are not a representation that the items offered are genuine items of the original Mfg.

Quality Replacement Parts

BRASS AMERICA

Quality Replacement Parts

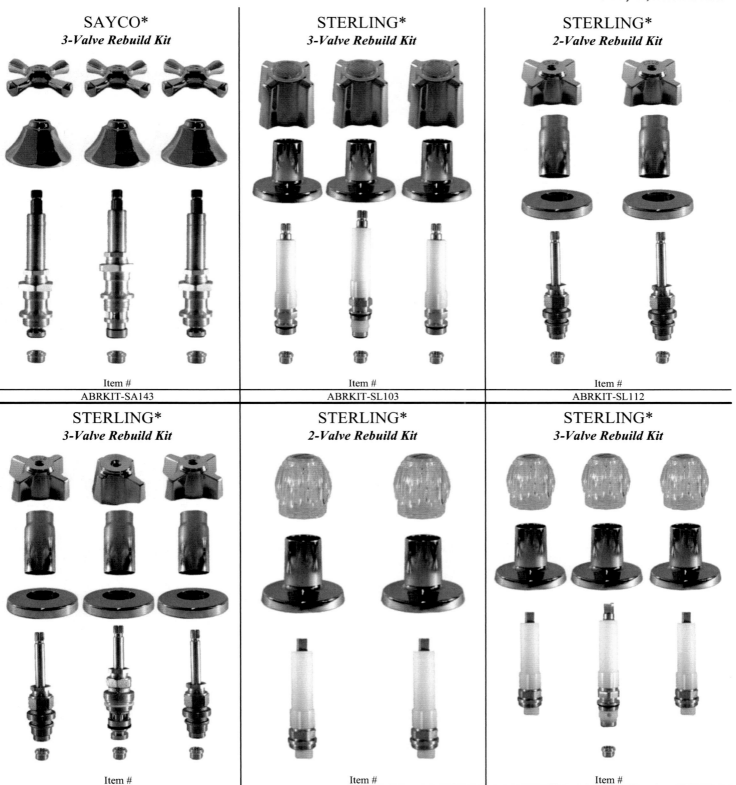

SAYCO*	STERLING*	STERLING*
3-Valve Rebuild Kit	*3-Valve Rebuild Kit*	*2-Valve Rebuild Kit*
Item #	Item #	Item #
ABRKIT-SA143	ABRKIT-SL103	ABRKIT-SL112
STERLING*	STERLING*	STERLING*
3-Valve Rebuild Kit	*2-Valve Rebuild Kit*	*3-Valve Rebuild Kit*
Item #	Item #	Item #
ABRKIT-SL113	ABRKIT-SL122	ABRKIT-SL123

To Order Call: 1.800.767.5552 . Fax: 1.800.886.9831

*Original Mfg's names are used for identification only and are not a representation that the items offered are genuine items of the original Mfg.   65

Quality Replacement Parts

STERLING*
2-Valve Rebuild Kit

Item #
ABRKIT-SL132

STERLING*
3-Valve Rebuild Kit

Item #
ABRKIT-SL133

STERLING*
2-Valve Rebuild Kit

Item #
ABRKIT-SL142

STERLING*
3-Valve Rebuild Kit

Item #
ABRKIT-SL143

STERLING*
3-Valve Rebuid Kit

Item #
ABRKIT-SL153

STERLING*
3-Valve Rebuild Kit

Item #
ABRKIT-SL163

To Order Call: 1.800.767.5552 . Fax: 1.800.886.9831

Original Mfg's names are used for identification only and are not a representation that the items offered are genuine items of the original Mfg.

Quality Replacement Parts

BRASS AMERICA
Quality Replacement Parts

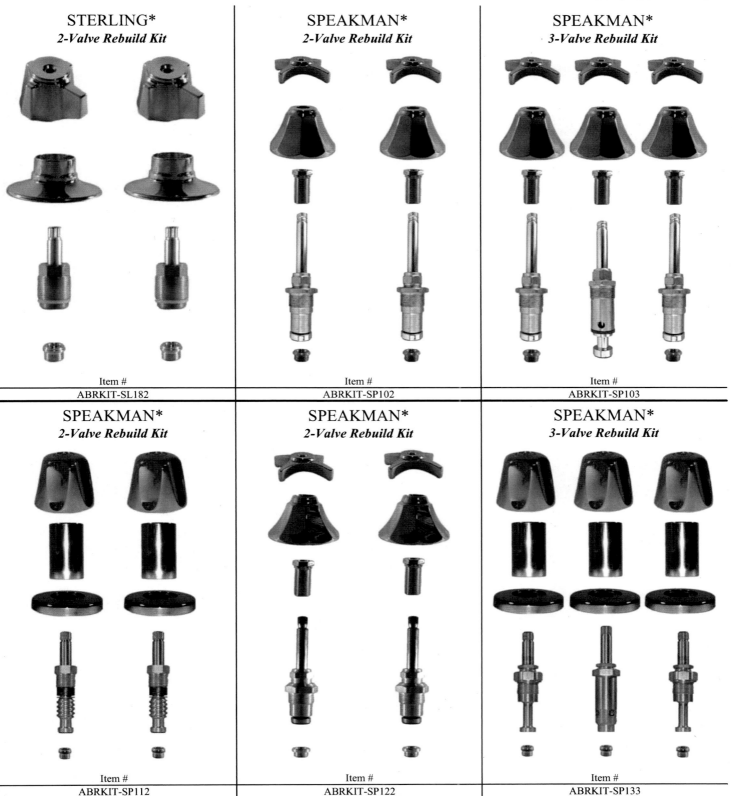

STERLING*	SPEAKMAN*	SPEAKMAN*
2-Valve Rebuild Kit	*2-Valve Rebuild Kit*	*3-Valve Rebuild Kit*

Item #	Item #	Item #
ABRKIT-SL182	ABRKIT-SP102	ABRKIT-SP103

SPEAKMAN*	SPEAKMAN*	SPEAKMAN*
2-Valve Rebuild Kit	*2-Valve Rebuild Kit*	*3-Valve Rebuild Kit*

Item #	Item #	Item #
ABRKIT-SP112	ABRKIT-SP122	ABRKIT-SP133

To Order Call: 1.800.767.5552 . Fax: 1.800.886.9831

Original Mfg's names are used for identification only and are not a representation that the items offered are genuine items of the original Mfg.

Quality Replacement Parts

SAVOY*
2-Valve Rebuild Kit

Item #
ABRKIT-SV102

SAVOY*
3-Valve Rebuild Kit

Item #
ABRKIT-SV103

SAVOY*
2-Valve Rebuid Kit

Item #
ABRKIT-SV112

SAVOY*
2-Valve Rebuild Kit

Item #
ABRKIT-SV122

SAVOY*
3-Valve Rebuild Kit

Item #
ABRKIT-SV123

SAVOY*
2-Valve Rebuild Kit

Item #
ABRKIT-SV132

To Order Call: 1.800.767.5552 . Fax: 1.800.886.9831

Original Mfg's names are used for identification only and are not a representation that the items offered are genuine items of the original Mfg.

Quality Replacement Parts

BRASS AMERICA
Quality Replacement Parts

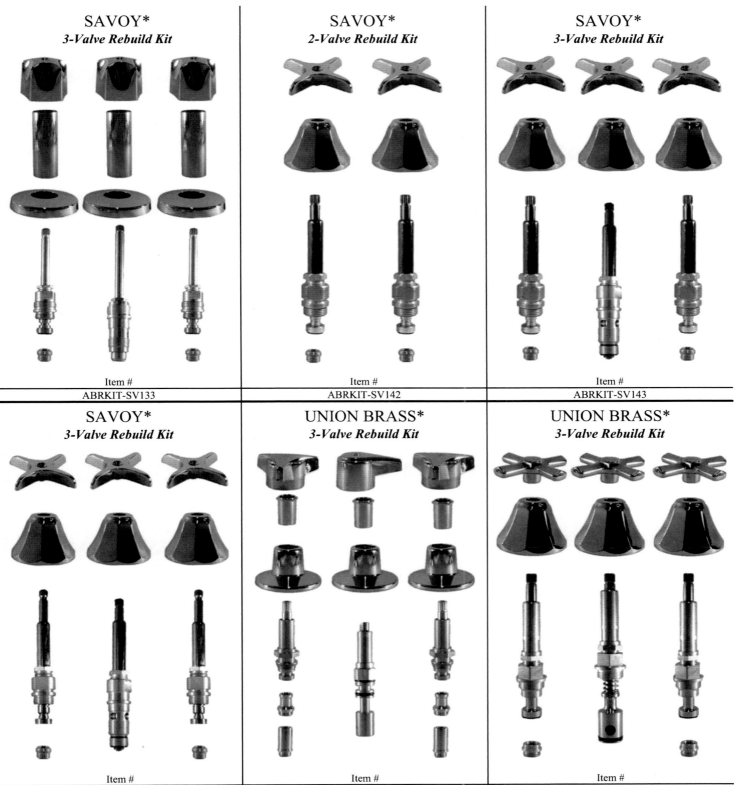

SAVOY*
3-Valve Rebuild Kit

Item #
ABRKIT-SV133

SAVOY*
2-Valve Rebuild Kit

Item #
ABRKIT-SV142

SAVOY*
3-Valve Rebuild Kit

Item #
ABRKIT-SV143

SAVOY*
3-Valve Rebuild Kit

Item #
ABRKIT-SV153

UNION BRASS*
3-Valve Rebuild Kit

Item #
ABRKIT-UN103

UNION BRASS*
3-Valve Rebuild Kit

Item #
ABRKIT-UN113

To Order Call: 1.800.767.5552 . Fax: 1.800.886.9831

69

Quality Replacement Parts

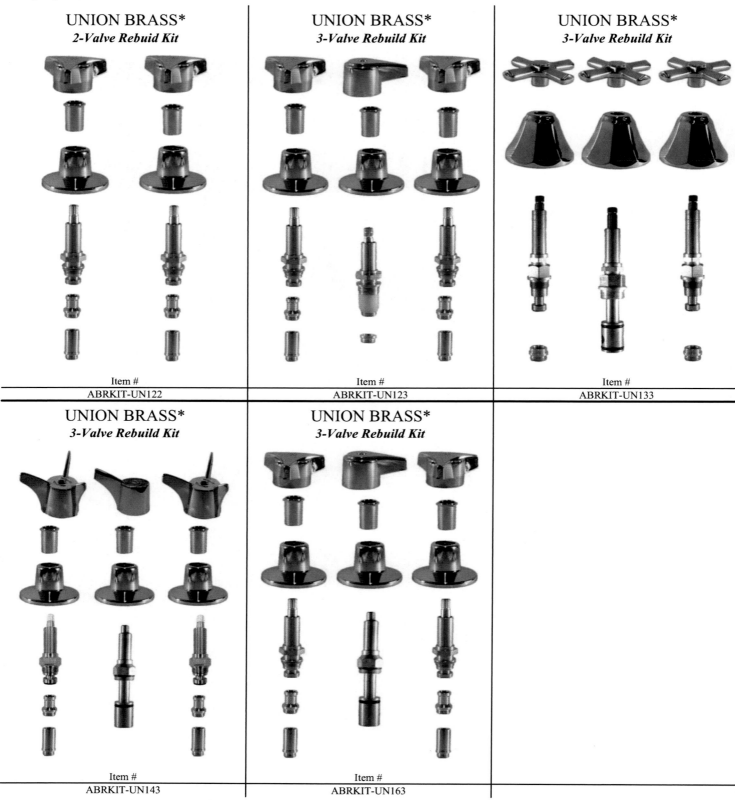

UNION BRASS*
2-Valve Rebuid Kit

Item #
ABRKIT-UN122

UNION BRASS*
3-Valve Rebuild Kit

Item #
ABRKIT-UN123

UNION BRASS*
3-Valve Rebuild Kit

Item #
ABRKIT-UN133

UNION BRASS*
3-Valve Rebuild Kit

Item #
ABRKIT-UN143

UNION BRASS*
3-Valve Rebuild Kit

Item #
ABRKIT-UN163

To Order Call: 1.800.767.5552 . Fax: 1.800.886.9831

Original Mfg's names are used for identification only and are not a representation that the items offered are genuine items of the original Mfg.

Index by Part Number

ABF1010-LF 43	ABFSBC-LF 44	ABRAB0502 40
ABF1010LP-LF 43	ABR1220DIV-LF 43	ABRAB0511 40
ABF1210-LF 43	ABR12C12CS 38	ABRAB0517 40
ABF1220-LF 43	ABR12F12CA-LF 38	ABRAB0534 40
ABF1410 43	ABR12F12CS 38	ABRAB0541 40
ABF2510DHLP-LF 43	ABR12F38CA-LF 38	ABRAB1165 44
ABF3013-LF 44	ABR12F38CS 38	ABRAB1200 38
ABF3050-LF 43	ABR1300DIV 37	ABRAB1201 38
ABF3055-LF 43	ABR1300DIVBOOT 37	ABRAB1211 39
ABF3057-LF 43	ABR3003 40	ABRAB1213 39
ABF3059-LF 44	ABR3057-HDL-PR 6	ABRAB1221 39
ABF3059-SPOUT-LF 44	ABR3057-STEM-PR-LF 6	ABRAB1224 39
ABF3060-LF 44	ABR3612-HOSE-LF 30	ABRAB1225 39
ABF3060-SPOUT-LF 44	ABR3612-SPRAY-LF 30	ABRAB1230 39
ABF3061-LF 44	ABR3612-SPRING 30	ABRAB1231 39
ABF3061-SPOUT-LF 44	ABR38C38CS-LF 38	ABRAB1240 39
ABF3104-LF 44	ABR38F38CA-LF 38	ABRAB1243 39
ABF3105-LF 44	ABR38F38CS 38	ABRAB1245 39
ABF3111-LF 44	ABR5371L-HDL 36	ABRAB1250 39
ABF3612-LF 44	ABR5510LS-HDL 36	ABRAB1308L 42
ABF4812 44	ABR5720DIV-LF 43	ABRAB133 42
ABF5310LS 43	ABR58C12CA 38	ABRAB134 42
ABF5371L 43	ABR58C38CA 38	ABRAB135 42
ABF5510 43	ABR58C38CA-LF 38	ABRAB191006 41
ABF5510LSB-LF 43	ABR58C38CS 38	ABRAB2035 41
ABF5510LSBSN-LF 43	ABR58C38CS-LF 38	ABRAB2055 41
ABF5510LSLP-LF 43	ABRAB038-2 40	ABRAB303 42
ABF5710LS-LF 43	ABRAB038-3 40	ABRAB32079-B 41
ABF5720LS-LF 43	ABRAB038-4 40	ABRAB32080-B 41

Index by Part Number

ABRAB40413 42	ABRAB9875 42	ABRAS32131 2
ABRAB40491 42	ABRAB9895 42	ABRAS32140 2
ABRAB453A 42	ABRAB9905 42	ABRAS32140D 2
ABRAB5110 42	ABRAB9925 42	ABRAS32141 2
ABRAB5120 39	ABRAM20176-LF 1	ABRAS32170 2
ABRAB5130 39	ABRAM20177 1	ABRAS32170D 2
ABRAB5211 39	ABRAM33051 1	ABRAS32171 2
ABRAB5213 39	ABRAM33051D 1	ABRAS32172 2
ABRAB5221-CTG 40	ABRAS10101-LF 1	ABRAS32172D 3
ABRAB5222-CTG 40	ABRAS10102-LF 1	ABRAS32173 3
ABRAB57130 41	ABRAS10103-LF 1	ABRAS32175 3
ABRAB57160 41	ABRAS10104-LF 1	ABRAS32176 3
ABRAB6011Z-1 40	ABRAS10105 1	ABRAS32178 3
ABRAB6011Z-2 40	ABRAS10108-LF 1	ABRAS32178D 3
ABRAB6011Z-3 40	ABRAS10109-LF 1	ABRAS32181 3
ABRAB6201 41	ABRAS20101 1	ABRAS32182 3
ABRAB7523 42	ABRAS20170-18T 1	ABRAS32183 3
ABRAB9605 42	ABRAS20172 1	ABRAS32183D 3
ABRAB9615 42	ABRAS20173 1	ABRAS32186 3
ABRAB9635 42	ABRAS20174 1	ABRAS32188 3
ABRAB9655 42	ABRAS20186-15 1	ABRAS32188D 3
ABRAB9675 42	ABRAS32100 1	ABRAS50329 3
ABRAB9695 42	ABRAS32101 2	ABRAS50344 3
ABRAB9705 42	ABRAS32101D 2	ABRAS50346 4
ABRAB9725 42	ABRAS32110 2	ABRAS50347 4
ABRAB9805 42	ABRAS32120 2	ABRAS50348 4
ABRAB9815 42	ABRAS32121 2	ABRAS50353-L 4
ABRAB9835 42	ABRAS32130 2	ABRAS50353-S 4
ABRAB9855 42	ABRAS32130D 2	ABRAS50354 4

Index by Part Number

Quality Replacement Parts

ABRAS77103C 4	ABRBV58C38CS 38	ABRCC19003 33
ABRAS77103D 4	ABRBV58C38CS-LF 38	ABRCC19006 33
ABRAS77103H 4	ABRCB10368-LF 6	ABRCC19008 33
ABRAS77104C 4	ABRCB10369-LF 5	ABRCC19010 33
ABRAS77104H 4	ABRCB10370-LF 5	ABRCC19011 33
ABRAS77179C 4	ABRCB10371-LF 5	ABRCC19012 33
ABRAS77179D 4	ABRCB20329 5	ABRCC19014 33
ABRAS77179H 4	ABRCB20331 5	ABRCC19015 33
ABRAS9001 4	ABRCB20332 5	ABRCC19016 34
ABRAS9002 4	ABRCB20333 5	ABRCC19017 34
ABRBP-10 44	ABRCB20336 5	ABRCC19019-LF 33
ABRBP-10-PVD 44	ABRCB20337 5	ABRCC19020-LF 33
ABRBR10213 4	ABRCB32231 5	ABRCC19023 34
ABRBR10213-GASKET 4	ABRCB32231D 5	ABRCC19023SP 34
ABRBR20251 4	ABRCB32232 5	ABRCC19024 34
ABRBR20252 4	ABRCB32233 6	ABRCC19025 34
ABRBR33246 4	ABRCB32240 6	ABRCC19026 34
ABRBR33651 5	ABRCB32240D 6	ABRCC19027 34
ABRBR33651D 5	ABRCB32241 6	ABRCC19028 34
ABRBR404-07 5	ABRCB32241C 6	ABRCC19029 34
ABRBV12F12CA 38	ABRCB32241H 6	ABRCC19030 34
ABRBV12F12CS 38	ABRCB33247 6	ABRCC19031 34
ABRBV12F38CA-LF 38	ABRCB50421 6	ABRCC19032 34
ABRBV12F38CS 38	ABRCBF360-3-LF 37	ABRCC19033 34
ABRBV12F38CS-LF 37	ABRCBF360-3-P 37	ABRCC19034 35
ABRBV58C12CA 38	ABRCBF360-KIT-LF 37	ABRCC19035 35
ABRBV58C12CS 38	ABRCBF360-LF 37	ABRCC19036 35
ABRBV58C12CS-LF 38	ABRCC19001 33	ABRCC19037 35
ABRBV58C38CA-LF 38	ABRCC19002 33	ABRCC19038 35

Index by Part Number

ABRCC19039 35	ABRCR32337 7	ABRDE33961 8
ABRCC19040 35	ABRCR32338 7	ABRDE404-01WA 8
ABRCC19041 35	ABRCR32339 7	ABRDE404-02 8
ABRCC19042 35	ABRCR32340 7	ABRDE404-03 8
ABRCC19043 35	ABRCR77121C 7	ABRDE408-04 8
ABRCC19044 35	ABRCR77121D 7	ABRDE408-16 8
ABRCC19045 35	ABRCR77121H 7	ABRDE50317 8
ABRCC19046 35	ABRCS100X075 41	ABRDE5200EX 8
ABRCC19047 35	ABRCS125 41	ABRDE7404-01 8
ABRCC19048 35	ABRCS150 41	ABRDE-KIT-1 9
ABRCC19049 36	ABRCS200 41	ABRDE-KIT-2 9
ABRCC-MIX 36	ABRCS200X125 41	ABRDL9200PCP 44
ABRCH10320 6	ABRCS200X150 41	ABRDLX-INDEX-C 8
ABRCH10320-LF 6	ABRCTG-LEV-COLD 37	ABRDLX-INDEX-H 8
ABRCH10321 6	ABRCTG-LEV-HOT 37	ABREL20524 9
ABRCH10321-LF 6	ABRDE10420 7	ABREL20525 9
ABRCH32001 6	ABRDE10421 7	ABREL20526 9
ABRCH32002 6	ABRDE10422 7	ABREL20527 9
ABRCH77180C 6	ABRDE10423 7	ABREL20528 9
ABRCH77180H 6	ABRDE10424 7	ABREL20529 9
ABRCPAERATOR-LF 37	ABRDE10426 7	ABREL20533 9
ABRCPI0503NS 40	ABRDE1-212B 9	ABREL33151 9
ABRCR10312-LF 6	ABRDE1-212B-LF 9	ABREL33152 9
ABRCR10313-LF 6	ABRDE1-212SS 9	ABREL33152D 9
ABRCR20334 6	ABRDE1-70B 8	ABREL33613 9
ABRCR20341 7	ABRDE1-70B-LF 8	ABREL33614 10
ABRCR32330 7	ABRDE1-70B-SP 8	ABREL33815 10
ABRCR32330D 7	ABRDE1-70SS 8	ABREL33820 10
ABRCR32335 7	ABRDE1-70SS-OEM 8	ABREL33820D 10

Index by Part Number

Quality Replacement Parts

ABRFA32235 10	ABRFA50325 12	ABRFA77161C 14
ABRFA32245 10	ABRFA50326 12	ABRFA77161C-PB 14
ABRFA32255 10	ABRFA50327 12	ABRFA77161D 14
ABRFA32266 10	ABRFA50330 12	ABRFA77161D-PB 14
ABRFA32267CP 10	ABRFA50331 12	ABRFA77161H 14
ABRFA32267PB 10	ABRFA50332 13	ABRFA77161H-PB 14
ABRFA32270 11	ABRFA50341-24T 13	ABRFA91620-L 14
ABRFA32271 11	ABRFA50350 13	ABRFA91620-S 14
ABRFA32410 11	ABRFA50351 13	ABRFEB091011 10
ABRFA32411 11	ABRFA50352 13	ABRFEB182512 10
ABRFA32412 11	ABRFA50361 13	ABRFEB19A 10
ABRFA32451 11	ABRFA50361-18T 13	ABRFEB19B 10
ABRFA32452 11	ABRFA50362 13	ABRFI32601 14
ABRFA32453 11	ABRFA50363 13	ABRFI32601C 14
ABRFA32480 11	ABRFA50372 13	ABRFI32601H 14
ABRFA32801 11	ABRFA50380 13	ABRGD-10 44
ABRFA32802 11	ABRFA5824S 14	ABRGD-10H 44
ABRFA33720 11	ABRFA77101C 13	ABRGE10724-LF 14
ABRFA33740 11	ABRFA77101D 13	ABRGE10725-LF 14
ABRFA33780 11	ABRFA77101H 13	ABRGE10726-LF 14
ABRFA408-10 12	ABRFA77102C 13	ABRGE10727-LF 14
ABRFA408-10L 12	ABRFA77102D 13	ABRGE20778B 14
ABRFA408-10S 12	ABRFA77102H 13	ABRGE20779 14
ABRFA50318 12	ABRFA77112C 13	ABRGE32500 14
ABRFA50320 12	ABRFA77112D 13	ABRGE32500D 14
ABRFA50321 12	ABRFA77112H 13	ABRGE32501 14
ABRFA50322 12	ABRFA77116C 13	ABRGE32501D 14
ABRFA50323 12	ABRFA77116D 13	ABRGE32510 14
ABRFA50324 12	ABRFA77116H 13	ABRGE32511 15

ABRGE32520 15	ABRIN33615D 16	ABRKIT-AS233 49
ABRGE32521D 15	ABRIN50384 16	ABRKIT-BR102 49
ABRGE32540 15	ABRKIT-AM102 45	ABRKIT-BR103 49
ABRGE32541 15	ABRKIT-AM103 45	ABRKIT-BR113 50
ABRGE32541D 15	ABRKIT-AM112 45	ABRKIT-BR122 50
ABRGE50377 15	ABRKIT-AM113 45	ABRKIT-BR123 50
ABRGE50403 15	ABRKIT-AR103 45	ABRKIT-CB102 50
ABRGE50437 15	ABRKIT-AR113 45	ABRKIT-CB103 50
ABRGE77122C 15	ABRKIT-AS102 46	ABRKIT-CB112 50
ABRGE77122D 15	ABRKIT-AS103 46	ABRKIT-CB113 51
ABRGE77122H 15	ABRKIT-AS112 46	ABRKIT-CB122 51
ABRHA20831 15	ABRKIT-AS113 46	ABRKIT-CB123 51
ABRHA20834 15	ABRKIT-AS122 46	ABRKIT-CB132 51
ABRHA32646 15	ABRKIT-AS123 46	ABRKIT-CB133 51
ABRHA32646D 15	ABRKIT-AS132 47	ABRKIT-CB142 51
ABRHA32647 15	ABRKIT-AS133 47	ABRKIT-CR102 52
ABRHA50340 16	ABRKIT-AS142 47	ABRKIT-CR103 52
ABRHA77176C 16	ABRKIT-AS143 47	ABRKIT-CR112 52
ABRHA77176H 16	ABRKIT-AS153 47	ABRKIT-CR113 52
ABRHA77177C 16	ABRKIT-AS162 47	ABRKIT-CR122 52
ABRHA77177D 16	ABRKIT-AS163 48	ABRKIT-CR132 52
ABRHA77177H 16	ABRKIT-AS172 48	ABRKIT-CR133 53
ABRIM13801-LF 33	ABRKIT-AS173 48	ABRKIT-CR142 53
ABRIM13802-LF 33	ABRKIT-AS182 48	ABRKIT-CR152 53
ABRIN20911 16	ABRKIT-AS183 48	ABRKIT-CR153 53
ABRIN20912 16	ABRKIT-AS192 48	ABRKIT-EL102 53
ABRIN33610 16	ABRKIT-AS193 49	ABRKIT-EL103 53
ABRIN33611 16	ABRKIT-AS222 49	ABRKIT-EL112 54
ABRIN33615 16	ABRKIT-AS232 49	ABRKIT-EL113 54

Index by Part Number

ABRKIT-EL123 54	ABRKIT-KO132 59	ABRKIT-PP193 64
ABRKIT-EL132 54	ABRKIT-KO133 59	ABRKIT-RY102 64
ABRKIT-EL133 54	ABRKIT-KO143 59	ABRKIT-SA102 64
ABRKIT-EL143 54	ABRKIT-KO152 59	ABRKIT-SA103 64
ABRKIT-EL152 55	ABRKIT-KO153 59	ABRKIT-SA113 64
ABRKIT-EL153 55	ABRKIT-KO162 60	ABRKIT-SA132 64
ABRKIT-GE102 55	ABRKIT-KO163 60	ABRKIT-SA143 65
ABRKIT-GE103 55	ABRKIT-KO172 60	ABRKIT-SL103 65
ABRKIT-GE112 55	ABRKIT-KO183 60	ABRKIT-SL112 65
ABRKIT-GE113 55	ABRKIT-MX101 60	ABRKIT-SL113 65
ABRKIT-GE122 56	ABRKIT-NI101 60	ABRKIT-SL122 65
ABRKIT-GE123 56	ABRKIT-PP102 61	ABRKIT-SL123 65
ABRKIT-GE142 56	ABRKIT-PP103 61	ABRKIT-SL132 66
ABRKIT-GE143 56	ABRKIT-PP112 61	ABRKIT-SL133 66
ABRKIT-GL103 56	ABRKIT-PP113 61	ABRKIT-SL142 66
ABRKIT-HA103 56	ABRKIT-PP122 61	ABRKIT-SL143 66
ABRKIT-HA152 57	ABRKIT-PP123 61	ABRKIT-SL153 66
ABRKIT-HA153 57	ABRKIT-PP132 62	ABRKIT-SL163 66
ABRKIT-HA162 57	ABRKIT-PP133 62	ABRKIT-SL182 67
ABRKIT-HA163 57	ABRKIT-PP142 62	ABRKIT-SP102 67
ABRKIT-IN102 57	ABRKIT-PP143 62	ABRKIT-SP103 67
ABRKIT-IN103 57	ABRKIT-PP152 62	ABRKIT-SP112 67
ABRKIT-IN113 58	ABRKIT-PP153 62	ABRKIT-SP122 67
ABRKIT-KO102 58	ABRKIT-PP162 63	ABRKIT-SP133 67
ABRKIT-KO103 58	ABRKIT-PP163 63	ABRKIT-SV102 68
ABRKIT-KO112 58	ABRKIT-PP172 63	ABRKIT-SV103 68
ABRKIT-KO113 58	ABRKIT-PP173 63	ABRKIT-SV112 68
ABRKIT-KO122 58	ABRKIT-PP182 63	ABRKIT-SV122 68
ABRKIT-KO123 59	ABRKIT-PP183 63	ABRKIT-SV123 68

Index by Part Number

ABRKIT-SV132 68	ABRKO21104 17	ABRMO21305 19
ABRKIT-SV133 69	ABRKO21111 17	ABRMO21305-LF............. 19
ABRKIT-SV142 69	ABRKO21112 17	ABRMO21306 19
ABRKIT-SV143 69	ABRKO21113 17	ABRMO32701 19
ABRKIT-SV153 69	ABRKO21114 17	ABRMO404-10L............... 20
ABRKIT-UN103 69	ABRKO21115 17	ABRMO404-10S............... 20
ABRKIT-UN113 69	ABRKO32630 17	ABRMO404-12L............... 20
ABRKIT-UN122 70	ABRKO32631 17	ABRMO404-12S............... 20
ABRKIT-UN123 70	ABRKO32632 17	ABRMO404-22L............... 20
ABRKIT-UN133 70	ABRKO32632D................. 17	ABRMW11323................. 18
ABRKIT-UN143 70	ABRKO32635 17	ABRMW11324................. 18
ABRKIT-UN163 70	ABRKO32636 17	ABRMW11325................. 18
ABRKO11101-LF............. 16	ABRKO32640 18	ABRMW11326................. 18
ABRKO11102-LF............. 16	ABRKO32641 18	ABRMW11327................. 18
ABRKO11124-LF............. 16	ABRKO32641D................. 18	ABRMW21323................. 19
ABRKO11125................. 16	ABRKO408-13 18	ABRMX21348-B 19
ABRKO11125-LF............. 16	ABRKO50366S 18	ABRMX34103............... 20, 36
ABRKO11126-LF............. 16	ABRKO50373 18	ABRMX404-16C............. 19
ABRKO11127-LF............. 16	ABRKO50381 18	ABRMX404-16S............. 19
ABRKO11128-LF............. 16	ABRKO50422 18	ABRMX404-17 19
ABRKO11134................. 16	ABRKO77131C................. 18	ABRMX404-18 19
ABRKO11134-LF............. 16	ABRKO77131D................. 18	ABRMX50337................. 19
ABRKO11135................. 16	ABRKO77131H................. 18	ABRNI11438 20
ABRKO11135-LF............. 16	ABRKO77132C................. 18	ABRNI11439 20
ABRKO11158................. 17	ABRKO77132H................. 18	ABRNI11440 20
ABRKO11159................. 17	ABRMO11300................. 19	ABRNI404-04 20
ABRKO21101................. 17	ABRMO11301................. 19	ABRNI408-14 20
ABRKO21102................. 17	ABRMO21304................. 19	ABRNI50336 20
ABRKO21103................. 17	ABRMO21304-LF 19	ABRNI50338 20

Index by Part Number

ABRNI50339 20	ABRPP21670.................... 22	ABRPP50412 24
ABRNI50343 20	ABRPP32800.................... 22	ABRPP50413 24
ABRPBAERATOR-LF 37	ABRPP32800D 22	ABRPP50414 24
ABRPBCV 36	ABRPP32803.................... 22	ABRPP704-09-1 24
ABRPBCV-CTG 36	ABRPP32811.................... 22	ABRPP77151C 24
ABRPBCV-MIX 36	ABRPP32840.................... 22	ABRPP77151D 24
ABRPBCV-RING 36	ABRPP32840D 22	ABRPP77151H 24
ABRPH11670-LF 20	ABRPP32841.................... 22	ABRPP77152C 24
ABRPH32760 20	ABRPP32850D 22	ABRPP77152D 24
ABRPH50328 21	ABRPP32860.................... 22	ABRPP77152H 24
ABRPH50333 21	ABRPP32870.................... 22	ABRPP77155C 24
ABRPH50334 21	ABRPP32870D 22	ABRPP77155D 24
ABRPP-01 44	ABRPP32880.................... 22	ABRPP77155H 24
ABRPP11635-LF 21	ABRPP32881.................... 22	ABRPP-SEAT................... 24
ABRPP11636-LF 21	ABRPP32882.................... 23	ABRSA11938-LF 25
ABRPP11637-LF 21	ABRPP32883.................... 23	ABRSA11939-LF 25
ABRPP11640 21	ABRPP32883D 23	ABRSA21951 25
ABRPP11641 21	ABRPP35132.................... 23	ABRSA21952 25
ABRPP11665-LF 21	ABRPP37156.................... 23	ABRSA21953 25
ABRPP11666-LF 21	ABRPP404-09................... 23	ABRSA21957 25
ABRPP11676-LF 21	ABRPP404-23L................. 23	ABRSA33030 25
ABRPP11691 21	ABRPP408-17................... 23	ABRSA33030D................. 25
ABRPP213218L 24	ABRPP408-17D 23	ABRSA33031 25
ABRPP21651 21	ABRPP408-19................... 23	ABRSA33031D................. 25
ABRPP21652 21	ABRPP408-20................... 23	ABRSA33033 26
ABRPP21653 21	ABRPP50342.................... 23	ABRSA33038 36
ABRPP21654 21	ABRPP50401.................... 23	ABRSA50371 26
ABRPP21655 21	ABRPP50402.................... 23	ABRSA50372 26
ABRPP21656 22	ABRPP50411.................... 24	ABRSA50391 26

Index by Part Number

ABRSA77162C 26	ABRSL33243D 27	ABRSPRAY-NOZZLE 37
ABRSA77162D 26	ABRSL33245 27	ABRSV21961 24
ABRSA77162H 26	ABRSL408-11 28	ABRSV21962 24
ABRSC6400 40	ABRSL408-11D 28	ABRSV21964 24
ABRSC6401 40	ABRSL408-12 28	ABRSV21968 24
ABRSC6421 40	ABRSL408-44 28	ABRSV21970 24
ABRSC6425 40	ABRSL408-44D 28	ABRSV21972 25
ABRSCP5120 39	ABRSL50366L 28	ABRSV32911 25
ABRSHOWER-ARM 40	ABRSL50375 28	ABRSV32911D 25
ABRSHOWER-ARM-8 40	ABRSL50376 28	ABRSV33248 25
ABRSL11965 26	ABRSL50388 28	ABRSV50368 25
ABRSL21981 26	ABRSL50423 28	ABRSV52912 25
ABRSL21982 26	ABRSL50424 28	ABRSW11911-LF 28
ABRSL21983 26	ABRSL77171C 28	ABRSW11912-LF 28
ABRSL21986 26	ABRSL77171D 28	ABRSW32900 29
ABRSL21987 26	ABRSL77171H 28	ABRSW33330 29
ABRSL21994 27	ABRSL77172C 28	ABRSY37210 29
ABRSL21995 27	ABRSL77172D 28	ABRSY37220 29
ABRSL32886 27	ABRSL77172H 28	ABRSY37221 29
ABRSL32890 27	ABRSL77173 28	ABRSY37230 29
ABRSL32890D 27	ABRSLEEVE-1410 43	ABRSY37231 29
ABRSL33210 27	ABRSP29200C 26	ABRSY37232 29
ABRSL33210D 27	ABRSP29200H 26	ABRSY77210 29
ABRSL33240 27	ABRSP33111 26	ABRTP-8120-C 42
ABRSL33241 27	ABRSP33111D 26	ABRTS12001-LF 29
ABRSL33241D 27	ABRSPM-100 42	ABRTS12002-LF 29
ABRSL33242 27	ABRSPM-200 42	ABRTS12007-LF 29
ABRSL33242D 27	ABRSPRAY-ESC 37	ABRTS12008-LF 29
ABRSL33243 27	ABRSPRAY-HOSE 37	ABRTS12009-LF 29

Index by Part Number

Quality Replacement Parts

ABRTS12010-LF 29	ABRUN33510DA 31	LF124640 37
ABRTS12013-LF 29	ABRUN33511 31	
ABRTS12014-LF 29	ABRUN33512 31	
ABRTS12015-LF 29	ABRUN33513D.................31	
ABRTS12016-LF 29	ABRUN33530 31	
ABRTS32953 29	ABRUN33531 31	
ABRTS32953D 30	ABRUN33532 31	
ABRTS32954 30	ABRUN50441 31	
ABRTS33410 30	ABRUN50442 31	
ABRTS33410C 30	ABRUN50443 31	
ABRTS33410H 30	ABRVA12241...................31	
ABRTS77178C 30	ABRVA12246...................31	
ABRTS77178H 30	ABRVA12247...................32	
ABRTS77190C 30	ABRVA12248...................32	
ABRTS77190H 30	ABRVA12249...................32	
ABRTSKIT-VB-LF............ 30	ABRVA33810...................32	
ABRUN12101-LF............. 30	ABRVA33811...................32	
ABRUN12102-LF............. 30	ABRVA404-15...................32	
ABRUN12156-LF............. 30	ABRVA404-21...................32	
ABRUN12157-LF............. 30	ABRVA408-01...................32	
ABRUN22109 30	ABRVA408-02...................32	
ABRUN22110 30	ABRVA704-20-1 32	
ABRUN22111 30	ABRVA7408-01BNC 32	
ABRUN22112 30	ABRVA7408-01BNH 32	
ABRUN22113 30	ABRVA-KIT1 32	
ABRUN22117 30	ABRWF32061 32	
ABRUN22119 31	FLAPBOX 41	
ABRUN33510 31	113740.............................42	
ABRUN33510D 31	LF124620........................37	

Index Button Cross Reference

Handle	Hot Button	Cold Button	Diverter Button
AM33051	PP77151H	PP77151C	
AM33051D			PP77151D
AS32100	AS77103H	AS77103C	
AS32101	AS77103H	AS77103C	
AS32101D			AS77103D
AS32110	AS77104H	AS77104C	
AS32140	FA77101H	FA77101C	
AS32140D			FA77101D
AS32141	FA77101H	FA77101C	
AS32170	FA77102H	FA77102C	
AS32170D			FA77102D
AS32171	FA77102H	FA77102C	
AS32183	FA77102H	FA77102C	
AS32183D			FA77102D
AS32186	ABRAS77115H	ABRAS77115C	
AS32188	ABRAS77179H	ABRAS77179C	
AS32188D			ABRAS77179D
BR33651	ABRAS77179H	ABRAS77179C	
BR33651D			ABRAS77179D
CR32335	CR77121H	CR77121C	
CR32335D			CR77121D
DE404-01WA	DE7404-01		
FA32235	FA77161H	FA77161C	FA77161D
FA32245	FA77101H	FA77101C	FA77101D
FA32266	FA77116H	FA77116C	FA77116D
FA32267CP	FA77116H	FA77116C	FA77116D
FA32267PB	139740-PB	139670-PB	
FA32410	FA77101H	FA77101C	FA77101D
FA32480	AS77103H	AS77103C	AS77103D
FA32801	FA77151H	FA77151C	FA77151D
FA32802	FA77151H	FA77151C	FA77151D
FA33780	SA77162H	SA77162C	SA77162D

Index Button Cross Reference

Handle	Hot Button	Cold Button	Diverter Button
FA408-10	SA77162H	SA77162C	SA77162D
FA408-10L	FA77112H	FA77112C	FA77112D
FA408-10S	FA77112H	FA77112C	FA77112D
GE32500	GE77122H	GE77122C	
GE32500D			GE77122D
GE32501	GE77122H	GE77122C	
GE32501D			GE77122D
GE32510	GE77122H	GE77122C	
GE32541	FA77101H	FA77101C	
GE32541D	FA77101H	FA77101C	FA77101D
HA32646	HA77177H	HA77177C	
HA32646D			HA77177D
HA32647	HA77176H	HA77176C	
KO32640	KO77131H	KO77131C	
KO32641	KO77131H	KO77131C	
KO32641D			KO77131D
NI408-14	FA77112H	FA77112C	
NI408-14D			FA77112D
PP32800	PP77151H	PP77151C	
PP32800D			PP77151D
PP32803	PP77152H	PP77152C	
PP32803D			PP77152D
PP32850D			PP77155D
PP32870	FA77101H	FA77101C	
PP32870D			FA77101D
PP32880	PP77155H	PP77155C	PP77155D
PP32881	PP77151H	PP77151C	
PP32883	PP77152H	PP77152C	
PP32883D			PP77152D
PP404-09	PP704-09-1		
PP404-23L	PP704-09-1		
PP408-17	CR77121H	CR77121C	

Index Button Cross Reference

Handle	Hot Button	Cold Button	Diverter Button
PP408-17D			CR77121D
PP408-19	CR77121H	CR77121C	
PP408-20	FA77101H	FA77101C	FA77101D
SA33030	SA77162H	SA77162C	
SA33030D			SA77162D
SA33031	SA77162H	SA77162C	
SA33031D			SA77162D
SA33033	SA77162H	SA77162C	
SL32890	FA77101H	FA77101C	
SL32890D			FA77101D
SL33210	SL77171H	SL77171C	
SL33210D			SL77171D
SL33242	SL77171H	SL77171C	
SL33242D			SL77171D
SL33243	SL77172H	SL77172C	
SL33243D			SL77172D
SL408-11	SL77172H	SL77172C	
SL408-11D			SL77172D
SL408-44	SL77172H	SL77172C	
SL408-44D			SL77172D
SP33111	FA77101H	FA77101C	
SP33111D			FA77101D
SY37210	SY77210		
TS32954	TS77178H	TS77178C	
VA12248	VA704-20-1		
VA408-01	VA7408-01BNC	VA7408-01BNH	
VA408-02	VA7408-01BNC	VA7408-01BNH	

CESCO BRASS

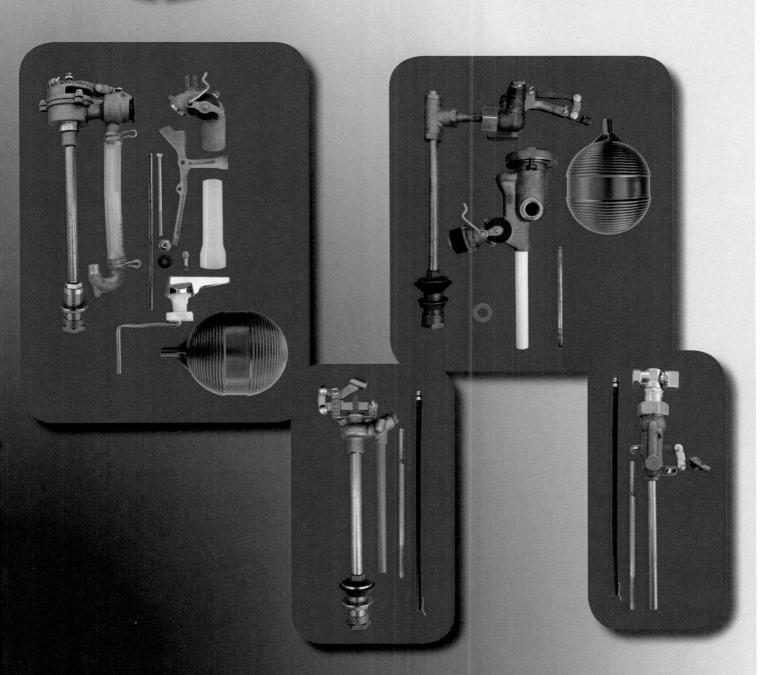

Table of Contents

o Briggs/Case* Parts 87

o Burlington Parts 91

o Scovill Parts 94

o Miscellaneous Parts 99

To Order Call: 1.800.767.5552 . Fax: 1.800.886.9831 . Online: www.cescobrass.com

86   *Original Mfg's names are used for identification only and are not a representation that the items offered are genuine items of the original Mfg.*

Model 50 For Briggs / Case

Item #
50

Repair Kits For Model 50 Briggs / Case

Plunger Repair Parts

Item #
SP-20

Vent Cap Replacement Parts

Item #
SP-24

Balcock Plunger

Item #
640320

Triple Seal Tank Ball

Item #
SP-69

To Order Call: 1.800.767.5552 . Fax: 1.800.886.9831 . Online: www.cescobrass.com

Original Mfg's names are used for identification only and are not a representation that the items offered are genuine items of the original Mfg. 87

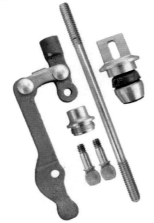

Repair Parts

Item #

SP-21

Regulator Replacement Parts

Item #

SP-23

Rim Valve Replacement Parts

Item #

SP-25

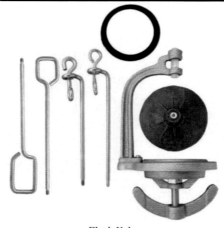

Vent Replacement Parts

Item #

SP-26

Flush Valve

Item #

SP-29

Replacement Parts

Item #

SP-32

Regulator & Stop Assembly

Item #

050-1129AA

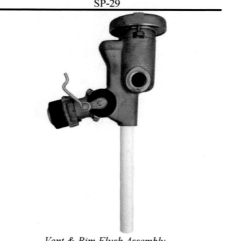

Vent & Rim Flush Assembly

Item #

050-1141A

Plunger Lever Assembly

Item #

050-1514A

Original Mfg's names are used for identification only and are not a representation that the items offered are genuine items of the original Mfg.

Model 62-8 For Briggs / Case

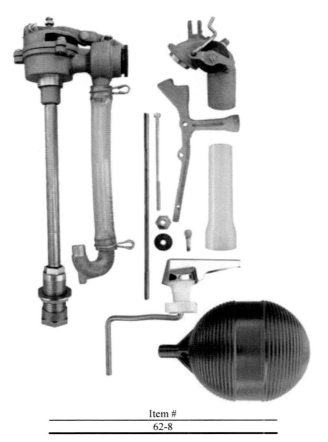

Item #
62-8

Repair Kits For Model 62-8 Briggs / Case

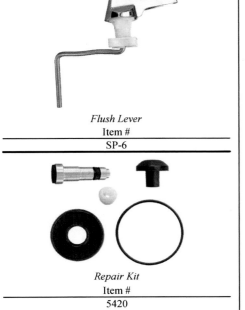

Flush Lever
Item #
SP-6

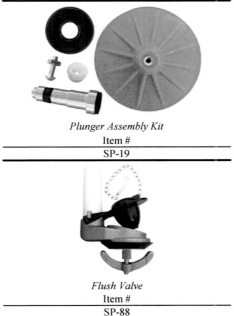

Plunger Assembly Kit
Item #
SP-19

Triple Seal Tank Ball
Item #
SP-69

Repair Kit
Item #
5420

Flush Valve
Item #
SP-88

Volume Control Regulator Assembly
Item #
062-5112A

To Order Call: 1.800.767.5552 . Fax: 1.800.886.9831 . Online: www.cescobrass.com

*Original Mfg's names are used for identification only and are not a representation that the items offered are genuine items of the origional Mfg. 89

Repair Kits For Model 62-8 Briggs / Case

Fill Valve Parts
Item #
SP-1

Diverter Valve Parts
Item #
SP-10

Pump Assembly
Item #
SP-12

Diverter Assembly
Item #
SP-30M

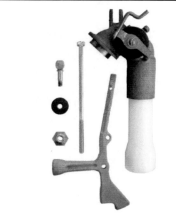

Diverter Valve Assembly
Item #
SP-61

Ballcock Valve Assembly
Item #
062-1211AA

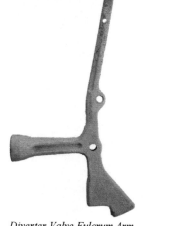

Diverter Valve Fulcrum Arm
Item #
062-1540

Ballcock Body Washer
Item #
000-6260

*Original Mfg's names are used for identification only and are not a representation that the items offered are genuine items of the original Mfg.

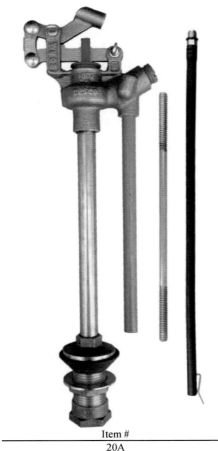

Item #
20A

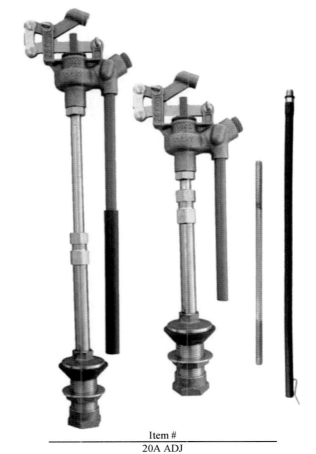

Item #
20A ADJ

Anti-Siphon Models	*Total Height in Tank*
20A	*10 1/4"*
20A XS	*9"*
20A MT	*11 1/4"*
20A XT	*12 1/4"*
20A ADJ	*9-13"*
Non Anti-Siphon Models	*Total Height in Tank*
20R	*10 1/4"*

1 13/16"

Regular Shank

2 47/64"

Long Shank

*For Long Shank add LS to end of part number
i.e. 20A LS*

To Order Call: 1.800.767.5552 . Fax: 1.800.886.9831 . Online: www.cescobrass.com

*Original Mfg's names are used for identification only and are not a representation that the items offered are genuine items of the original Mfg.   **91**

Repair Kit for 15A & 20A with Lever Assembly
Item #
1520ARK

Repair Kit for 15A & 20A
Item #
1520ARP

Old Style Repair Kit for 15 & 20R
Item #
1520RP

New Style Repair Kit for 16 & 20R
Item #
1436ARP

Plunger Assembly for New Style 15 & 20R
Item #
000-1436PA

Plunger Assembly for 15A & 20A
Item #
000-1437PB

Plunger Assembly for New Style 20A
Item #
000-1437PA

Lever Assembly for 15, 20R & 20A
Item #
000-1510A

To Order Call: 1.800.767.5552 . Fax: 1.800.886.9831 . Online: www.cescobrass.com

Original Mfg's names are used for identification only and are not a representation that the items offered are genuine items of the original Mfg.

Seat Washer
Item #
000-2868D

Seat for Old Style 15 & 20R
Item #
000-6021

Seat for New Style 15, 20R & 20A
Item #
000-6023

U-Cup ($\frac{5}{8}$ x $\frac{3}{8}$ x $\frac{1}{8}$)
Item #
000-8024A

Brass Regulator
Item #
020-5108

Regulator Assembly for 20R & 20A
Item #
020-5108PA

Sealing Ball $\frac{1}{2}$"
Item #
000-0050

Plunger Cup Washer for Old Style 15 & 20R
Item #
000-2863

To Order Call: 1.800.767.5552 . Fax: 1.800.886.9831 . Online: www.cescobrass.com

*Original Mfg's names are used for identification only and are not a representation that the items offered are genuine items of the original Mfg.
93

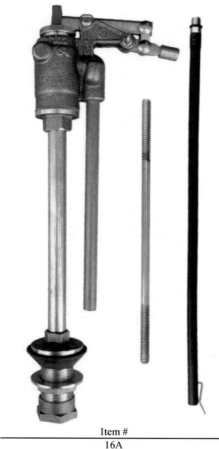

Item #
16A

Item #
16A ADJ

Anti-Siphon Models	Total Height in Tank
16A	10 1/4"
16A MT	11 1/4"
16A XT	12 1/4"
16A ADJ	9-13"
Non Anti-Siphon Models	Total Height in Tank
16	10 1/4"

1 13/16"

Regular Shank

2 47/64"

Long Shank

*For Long Shank add LS to end of part number
i.e. 16A LS*

To Order Call: 1.800.767.5552 . Fax: 1.800.886.9831 . Online: www.cescobrass.com

94 *Original Mfg's names are used for identification only and are not a representation that the items offered are genuine items of the original Mfg.*

Scovill Model 47130VB Ballcock for American Standard*

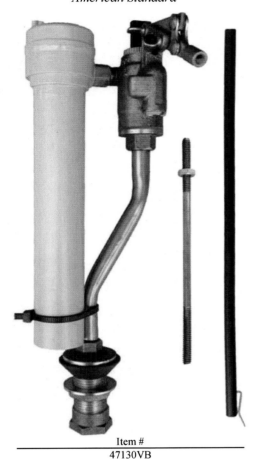

Item #
47130VB

Replacement for American Standard* Models
47130* & 47131* Ballcocks in the following toilets
(with tank numbers):
"Lexington"* (2006 & 2007)
"Ellisse"* (2008)

Scovill Model 16AK Anit-Siphon Ballcock for Kohler*

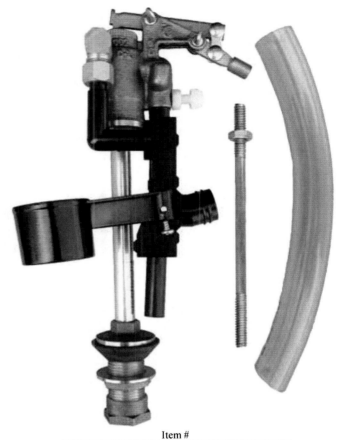

Item #
16AK

Replacement for Kohler* Models 43130* & 30673*
Ballcocks in the following toilets
(with tank numbers):
"Rialto"* (3402)
"Palarre"* (3383)
"San Raphael"* (3397)
"Rochelle"* (3385)
"Pillow Talk"* (3378)
"Cabernet"* (3401 & 3408)

To Order Call: 1.800.767.5552 . Fax: 1.800.886.9831 . Online: www.cescobrass.com

*Original Mfg's names are used for identification only and are not a representation that the items offered are genuine items of the original Mfg.   95

Scovill Model 12
Back Supply Float Valve

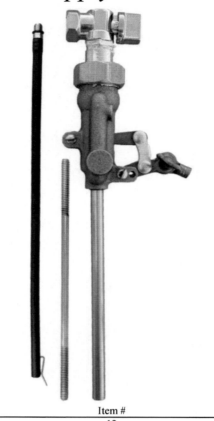

Item #
12

Scovill Repair Kits & Parts

Repair Kit for Model 12
Item #
12RP

Repair Kit for Model 12 with Plunger
Item #
12RPA

Repair Kit for Models 16A & S20OA
Item #
16200ARP

Repair Kit for Model 16AK
Item #
16AKRP

Repair Kit for Old Style Models 16 & 20S
Item #
16S200RP

Plunger Assembly for Models 16 & VB47130
Item #
000-8729BA

To Order Call: 1.800.767.5552 . Fax: 1.800.886.9831 . Online: www.cescobrass.com

96 *Original Mfg's names are used for identification only and are not a representation that the items offered are genuine items of the original Mfg.*

Plunger Assembly with Ball for Model 16
Item #
000-8729CA

Plunger Assembly with Ball for Model 16A
Item #
000-8729PB

U-Cup ($9/16$ x $3/16$ x $1/8$) for All Model 16's & VB
Item #
000-8730A

Seat Washer for Models 16, S200 & VB
Item #
000-8684D

Nylon Seat for All Model 16's, 12 & VB
Item #
000-8725

Rim Feed Tube for Model 16AK
Item #
016-0100K

Lever Assembly for All Model 16's
Item #
016-8792A

Regulator for All Model 16's
Item #
016-8600S

Diverter Valve for Model 16AK
Item #
016-3413A

$3/8$ x $3/8$ Ball Valve for Model 12
Item #
012-8212A

Shut-Off Assembley for Model 12
Item #
012-8212AA

Plunger Lever Assembly for Model 12
Item #
012-8224A

To Order Call: 1.800.767.5552 . Fax: 1.800.886.9831 . Online: www.cescobrass.com

*Original Mfg's names are used for identification only and are not a representation that the items offered are genuine items of the original Mfg. 97

Plunger Assembly for Model 12
Item #
012-8225A

Seat Washer for Model 12
Item #
012-8228

U-Cup ($\frac{3}{4}$ x $\frac{1}{2}$ x $\frac{1}{8}$) for Model 12
Item #
012-8247

Brass Plunger Assembly for Model 16AK
Item #
000-8728KA

Brass Plunger Assembly for Model 16
Item #
000-8729AA

Plunger Assembly for Model 16A
Item #
000-8729PA

Seat for Model 16AK
Item #
000-6021

Original Mfg's names are used for identification only and are not a representation that the items offered are genuine items of the original Mfg.

Ballcock Long Shank
Item #
000-1911

Ballcock Shank
Item #
000-1929

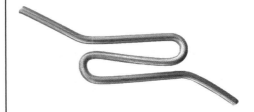

Stainless Steel Clip
Item #
000-3730

Sealing Ball ⅜"
Item #
000-0038

Brass Thumbscrew
Item #
000-3017

Coupling Nut Fiber Washer
Item #
000-2829

Cone Shank Washer
Item #
000-2812

Locknut
Item #
000-7113

Coupling Nut ½" Style
Item #
000-7116

Duckbill Check Valve
Item #
657-2829

Cesco Model 45 Tank Float Ball 4" x 5"
Item #
45

Compression Stop ⅜" x ⅜"
Item #
038-0038

To Order Call: 1.800.767.5552 . Fax: 1.800.886.9831 . Online: www.cescobrass.com

Original Mfg's names are used for identification only and are not a representation that the items offered are genuine items of the original Mfg.   **99**

Ballcock Shank-Mounted Quarter Stop Turn
Item #
038-1516A

10" Vinyl Refill Tube Assembly
Item #
000-2095C

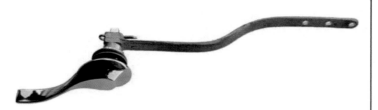

Scovill Model 92 Tank Lever
Item #
92

Scovill Model 93 Universal Tank Lever (Heavy Duty)
Item #
93

Burlington Model 100 Tank Lever
Item #
100

Universal Fit Model 101 Tank Lever
Item #
101

Float Rods

Item #	Length
050-2108	5"
000-7006	6"
000-7007	7"
000-2123	8"
000-2103	9"
000-2113	10"

To Order Call: 1.800.767.5552 . Fax: 1.800.886.9831 . Online: www.cescobrass.com

100 *Original Mfg's names are used for identification only and are not a representation that the items offered are genuine items of the original Mfg.*

Made in the USA
Monee, IL
24 May 2024

58539551R00067